Higher
Maths

PAST PAPER SOLUTIONS

2007/08 Edition

Steven O'Hagan
George Kinnear

Higher Still Notes

ISBN: 978 0 9557067 0 7

Published by Higher Still Notes
www.hsn.uk.net

Note: The contents of this book have not been checked or approved by the Scottish Qualifications Authority. They reflect the authors' opinion of good answers to exam questions, and where possible have been checked against publicly available marking instructions.

Printed by Bell & Bain Ltd., Glasgow, Scotland, UK.

Contents

Introduction

How to use this book

Past papers are probably the best practice you can get for the actual exam, so you should plan to do as many as possible. Make sure you practice doing a whole paper in the allocated time, so you can get used to the pace.

The best way to use this book is for checking your answers *after* you have tried the questions yourself. Don't just read the solutions whenever you get stuck!

Here are some features of the book which should help you:

Questions and parts

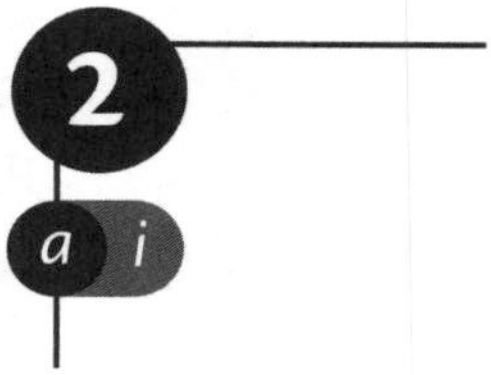

The question number is shown in the big circle, making it easy to spot at a glance.

All the parts of the question, including subparts, are also labelled.

References to notes

The grey box at the start of each solution has pointers to useful sections of our free Higher Maths notes (see below for details).

The "§" symbol just means "section", so the example to the right says you should look up Section 3 in the notes for Integration.

Clouds

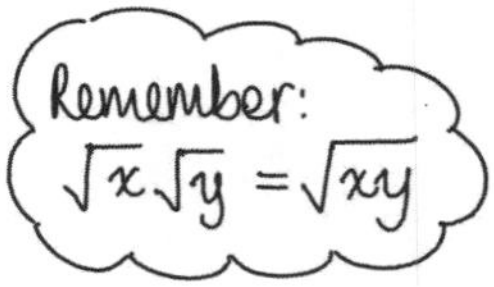

You'll notice these in a lot of solutions.

They usually contain helpful reminders, or explanations of the steps in the working.

Get more help with Higher Maths

You can download a free set of Higher Maths notes on our website:

www.hsn.uk.net/Higher-Maths

and you can also join our online forum, where you can chat with other students and ask about any questions you're stuck on:

www.hsn.uk.net/forum

Frequency Grid

	2003		2004		2005		2006		2007		SQP	
	P1	P2	P1	P2	P1	P2	P1	P2	P1	P2	P1	P2
Straight Lines	1		1	1	1	3a	1	1	1			1
Functions and Graphs	9	2, 5, 11a	4		4, 7b		3	7	3	4a	2, 6, 17	
Differentiation	5	4a, 8	8b	5, 7, 9	8c	6		3a, 12	9	5a, 6	1, 22	4a, 5b
Sequences	4			4	6		4		7		5, 21	
Polynomials and Quadratics	2, 7, 11b	1	2, 8a, 11a	3	8a,b	11	8, 9b,c	2, 3b	4, 8a,b	5b, 10a	7, 12, 14, 23	
Integration		3	11b	11		1, 5	6	5	8c	10b	3, 13	5a
Trigonometry	10	10	3, 10		9	2, 8	7	8	6	2, 4b	8, 9, 24	7
Circles	11a	4b		8	2, 11	3b,c	2	4	5	3, 5c	10, 15	4b
Vectors	3, 6	9	5	2	3	4, 10	9a,d	6	2	1	4, 11, 18	2, 4c
Further Calculus	8	6	6, 7		5		5	9, 10b	10	7	16	
Exponentials and Logarithms	12	11b	9	10	7a	7, 9	10	11		8, 9, 11	19, 20	6
Wave Functions		7		6	10			10a	11			3

Formulae List

Circle

The equation $x^2 + y^2 + 2gx + 2fy + c = 0$ represents a circle centre $(-g, -f)$ and radius $\sqrt{g^2 + f^2 - c}$.

The equation $(x-a)^2 + (y-b)^2 = r^2$ represents a circle centre (a, b) and radius r.

Scalar Product

$\boldsymbol{a}.\boldsymbol{b} = |\boldsymbol{a}||\boldsymbol{b}|\cos\theta$ where θ is the angle between $\boldsymbol{a}$ and $\boldsymbol{b}$.

or $\boldsymbol{a}.\boldsymbol{b} = a_1b_1 + a_2b_2 + a_3b_3$ where $\boldsymbol{a} = \begin{pmatrix} a_1 \\ a_2 \\ a_3 \end{pmatrix}$ and $\boldsymbol{b} = \begin{pmatrix} b_1 \\ b_2 \\ b_3 \end{pmatrix}$.

Trigonometric formulae

$$\sin(A \pm B) = \sin A \cos B \pm \cos A \sin B$$

$$\cos(A \pm B) = \cos A \cos B \mp \sin A \sin B$$

$$\sin 2A = 2 \sin A \cos A$$

$$\begin{aligned} \cos 2A &= \cos^2 A - \sin^2 A \\ &= 2\cos^2 A - 1 \\ &= 1 - 2\sin^2 A \end{aligned}$$

Table of standard derivatives

$f(x)$	$f'(x)$
$\sin ax$	$a\cos ax$
$\cos ax$	$-a\sin ax$

Table of standard integrals

$f(x)$	$\int f(x)\,dx$
$\sin ax$	$-\frac{1}{a}\cos ax + c$
$\cos ax$	$\frac{1}{a}\sin ax + c$

2003 Paper 1

1

See **Straight Lines** §5 and §6

$4x + y - 1 = 0$

$y = -4x + 1$

$m = -4$ so $m_{\perp} = \frac{1}{4}$.

Remember:
To extract the gradient, rearrange to the form $y = mx + c$.

The equation of the line is:

$y - 3 = \frac{1}{4}(x - (-1))$ using point $(-1, 3)$.

$4y - 12 = x + 1$ multiplying by 4.

$x - 4y + 13 = 0$.

2

See **Polynomials and Quadratics** – (a) §3, (b) §4

a <u>Method 1</u> $f(x) = x^2 + 6x + 11 = (x+3)^2 - 9 + 11 = (x+3)^2 + 2$.

This gives the correct x^2 and x terms, and an extra 9.

Take off this extra 9.

<u>Method 2</u> Comparing coefficients...

$x^2 + 6x + 11 = (x+a)^2 + b$

$= x^2 + 2ax + a^2 + b$

So $2a = 6$ and $a^2 + b = 11$

$a = 3$ $\quad$ $b = 11 - 3^2$

$= 2$.

So $f(x) = (x+3)^2 + 2$.

cont...

b The parabola has turning point $(-3, 2)$.
The parabola is concave up (U-shaped) since the x^2-coefficient is positive.
Also, when $x = 0$, $y = 11$.

Remember:
The parabola $y = (x-p)^2 + q$ has turning point (p, q).

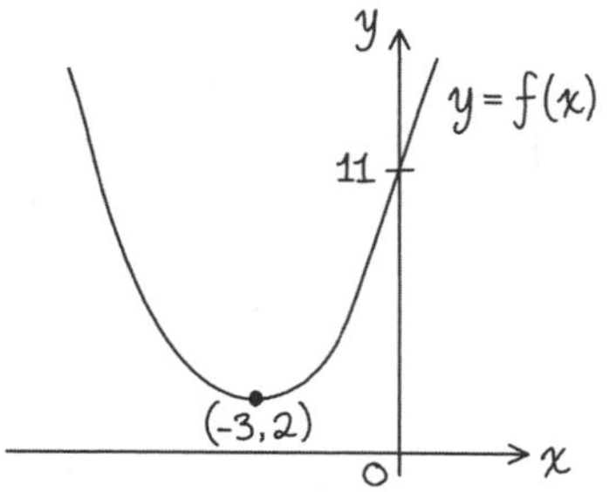

3

See **Vectors** §13

$$\underline{u}.\underline{v} = 3 \times 2 + 2 \times (-3) + 0 \times 4$$
$$= 6 - 6$$
$$= 0.$$

So $\underline{u}$ and $\underline{v}$ are perpendicular.

Remember:
$\underline{u}.\underline{v} = 0$
$\Leftrightarrow$ $\underline{u}$ and $\underline{v}$ are perpendicular.

4

See **Sequences** – (a) §5, (b) §4

a $u_1 = pu_0 + q$ $\qquad$ $u_2 = pu_1 + q$

$15 = 12p + q$ —— ① $\qquad$ $16 = 15p + q$ —— ②

② − ①: $1 = 3p$ i.e. $p = \frac{1}{3}$.

$q = 15 - 12 \times \frac{1}{3}$ using ①
$= 15 - 4$
$= 11.$

cont...

b Since $-1 < p < 1$, the sequence has a limit.

Method 1 $\quad l = \frac{q}{1-p} = \frac{11}{1-\frac{1}{3}} = \frac{11}{\frac{2}{3}} = \frac{33}{2}$ (or $16\frac{1}{2}$).

Method 2 $\quad$ As $n \to \infty$, $u_{n+1} = u_n = l$:

$$l = \tfrac{1}{3}l + 11$$
$$\tfrac{2}{3}l = 11$$
$$l = \tfrac{33}{2} \text{ (or } 16\tfrac{1}{2}\text{)}.$$

5

See **Differentiation** §2 and §4

$$f(x) = x^{\frac{1}{2}} + 2x^{-2}.$$

$$f'(x) = \tfrac{1}{2}x^{-\frac{1}{2}} - 4x^{-3} = \frac{1}{2\sqrt{x}} - \frac{4}{x^3}.$$

$$f'(4) = \frac{1}{2\sqrt{4}} - \frac{4}{4^3} = \frac{1}{4} - \frac{1}{16} = \frac{4}{16} - \frac{1}{16} = \frac{3}{16}.$$

6

See **Vectors** §10

From the diagram $\vec{AD} = 3\vec{AB}$, so...

$$\underline{d} - \underline{a} = 3(\underline{b} - \underline{a})$$
$$\underline{d} = 3\underline{b} - 3\underline{a} + \underline{a}$$
$$= 3\underline{b} - 2\underline{a}$$
$$= 3\begin{pmatrix}2\\-1\\1\end{pmatrix} - 2\begin{pmatrix}-1\\-3\\2\end{pmatrix}$$
$$= \begin{pmatrix}6\\-3\\3\end{pmatrix} - \begin{pmatrix}-2\\-6\\4\end{pmatrix}$$
$$= \begin{pmatrix}8\\3\\-1\end{pmatrix} \quad \text{So D is } (8, 3, -1).$$

7

See **Polynomials and Quadratics** §7

At points of intersection...

$$2x + 1 = x^2 + 3x + 4.$$

$$x^2 + x + 3 = 0$$

The discriminant is $b^2 - 4ac = 1^2 - 4 \times 1 \times 3$ using: $a = 1$, $b = 1$, $c = 3$

$$= -11 < 0.$$

Since $b^2 - 4ac < 0$, there are no solutions, so there are no points of intersection.

8

See **Further Calculus** §5

$$\int_0^1 (3x+1)^{-1/2}\,dx = \left[\frac{(3x+1)^{1/2}}{\frac{1}{2} \times 3}\right]_0^1$$

$$= \left[\frac{2}{3}\sqrt{3x+1}\right]_0^1$$

$$= \frac{2}{3}\sqrt{4} - \frac{2}{3}\sqrt{1}$$

$$= \frac{4}{3} - \frac{2}{3}$$

$$= \frac{2}{3}.$$

Remember: $\int (ax+b)^n dx = \frac{(ax+b)^{n+1}}{a(n+1)} + c$

9

See **Functions and Graphs** – *(a)* §3, *(b)* §2

a $h(x) = f(g(x))$

$$= f(2x+3)$$

$$= \frac{1}{2x+3-4}$$

$$= \frac{1}{2x-1}$$

b $2x - 1 \neq 0$

$$x \neq \frac{1}{2}.$$

Remember: It is impossible to divide by zero.

10

See **Trigonometry** §3 and §4

$\sqrt{8^2+4^2} = \sqrt{80}$

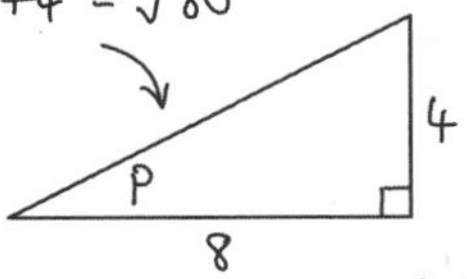

a i

$$\sin 2p = 2\sin p\cos p$$
$$= 2 \times \frac{4}{\sqrt{80}} \times \frac{8}{\sqrt{80}}$$
$$= \frac{64}{80}$$
$$= \frac{4}{5}$$

$$\sin p = \frac{\text{opp.}}{\text{hyp.}} = \frac{4}{\sqrt{80}}$$
$$\cos p = \frac{\text{adj.}}{\text{hyp.}} = \frac{8}{\sqrt{80}}$$

ii **Method 1** $\sin 2p = \frac{\text{opp.}}{\text{hyp.}} = \frac{4}{5}$. So we have:

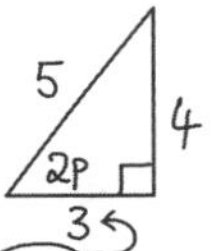

So $\cos 2p = \frac{\text{adj.}}{\text{hyp.}} = \frac{3}{5}$.

Using Pythagoras's Theorem.

Method 2

$$\cos 2p = 2\cos^2 p - 1$$
$$= 2\times\left(\frac{8}{\sqrt{80}}\right)^2 - 1$$
$$= 2 \times \frac{64}{80} - 1$$
$$= 2 \times \frac{4}{5} - 1$$
$$= \frac{8}{5} - \frac{5}{5}$$
$$= \frac{3}{5}$$

Any of the three formulae for cos2p could be used.

b $m_{OB} = \tan 2p = \frac{4}{3}$ using the diagram in Method 1 above.

OR $\tan 2p = \frac{\sin 2p}{\cos 2p} = \frac{4/5}{3/5} = \frac{4}{3}$.

2003

11

(a) See **Circles** *§1 and* **Polynomials and Quadratics** *§4*
(b) See **Polynomials and Quadratics** *§5*

a i $(x-12)^2+(y+5)^2=25$ has centre $A(12,-5)$.

$OA=\sqrt{12^2+(-5)^2}=\sqrt{144+25}=\sqrt{169}=13$

ii The turning point of the parabola is A. This lies halfway between the roots, so B is $(24,0)$.

Radius = OA – radius of small circle.
$= 13-5$
$= 8$.

So the equation of the circle is...

$$(x-24)^2+y^2=8^2$$
$$(x-24)^2+y^2=64.$$

b The parabola has roots $x=0$ and $x=24$. So its equation has the form $y=px(x-24)$, i.e. $q=-24$.

Since $A(12,-5)$ lies on the parabola...

$$-5=12p(12-24)$$
$$-5=-144p$$
$$p=\frac{5}{144}.$$

So $p=\frac{5}{144}$ and $q=-24$.

12

See **Exponentials and Logarithms** §4

Method 1 $3\log_e(2e) - 2\log_e(3e)$

$= 3(\log_e 2 + \underbrace{\log_e e}_{1}) - 2(\log_e 3 + \underbrace{\log_e e}_{1})$

$= 3\log_e 2 + 3 - 2\log_e 3 - 2$

$= 1 + \log_e 2^3 - \log_e 3^2$

$= 1 + \log_e 8 - \log_e 9.$

Remember:
- $\log_a xy = \log_a x + \log_a y$
- $\log_a a = 1.$
- $\log_a x^k = k\log_a x$

Method 2 $3\log_e(2e) - 2\log_e(3e)$

$= \log_e(2e)^3 - \log_e(3e)^2$

$= \log_e 8 + \underbrace{\log_e e^3}_{3} - \log_e 9 - \underbrace{\log_e e^2}_{2}$

$= 1 + \log_e 8 - \log_e 9.$

2003 Paper 2

1

See **Polynomials and Quadratics** §9

a Evaluate $f(2)$...

2	6	−5	−17	6
		12	14	−6
	6	7	−3	0

OR
$$f(2) = 6\times 2^3 - 5\times 2^2 - 17\times 2 + 6$$
$$= 6\times 8 - 5\times 4 - 34 + 6$$
$$= 48 - 20 - 34 + 6$$
$$= 0.$$

Since $f(2) = 0$, $x = 2$ is a root and so $(x-2)$ is a factor.

b $f(x) = (x-2)(6x^2 + 7x - 3)$
$= (x-2)(2x+3)(3x-1)$.

Either from the bottom row of the table or by inspection.

2

See **Functions and Graphs** §9 and §10

The amplitude is $\frac{\text{max} - \text{min}}{2} = \frac{5+3}{2} = 4$. So $a = 4$.

There are 2 complete waves in 2π radians, so $b = 2$.

The curve is the same as $y = 4\sin 2x$ shifted up 1 place.
So $c = 1$.

3

See **Integration** §6

The shaded area is

$$\int_0^4 (\text{upper} - \text{lower})\,dx = \int_0^4 \left(x^2 + 2x - (x^3 - x^2 - 6x)\right)dx$$
$$= \int_0^4 \left(-x^3 + 2x^2 + 8x\right)dx$$
$$= \left[-\tfrac{1}{4}x^4 + \tfrac{2}{3}x^3 + 4x^2\right]_0^4$$
$$= -4^3 + \frac{2\times 64}{3} + 4^3$$
$$= \frac{128}{3} \left(\text{or } 42\tfrac{2}{3}\right) \text{ square units.}$$

4

(a) See **Differentiation** §5
(b) See **Circles** §5

a When $x = 1$, $y = 1^3 + 2\times 1^2 - 3\times 1 + 2 = 2$. $(1,2)$.

$\frac{dy}{dx} = 3x^2 + 4x - 3$. When $x = 1$, $\frac{dy}{dx} = 4$.

Remember: $\frac{dy}{dx} = m_{tangent}$.

The equation of the tangent is

$$y - 2 = 4(x - 1)$$
$$y - 2 = 4x - 4$$
$$4x - y - 2 = 0.$$

b To find point of intersection, put $y = 4x - 2$ into the equation of the circle:

$$x^2 + (4x-2)^2 - 12x - 10(4x-2) + 44 = 0$$
$$x^2 + 16x^2 - 16x + 4 - 12x - 40x + 20 + 44 = 0$$
$$17x^2 - 68x + 68 = 0$$
$$x^2 - 4x + 4 = 0$$
$$(x-2)^2 = 0.$$
$$x = 2.$$

You could also use the discriminant to show that there is only one solution.

Since there is only one point of intersection, the line is a tangent to the circle. When $x = 2$, $y = 4\times 2 - 2 = 6$. So the point of contact is $(2,6)$.

5

See **Functions and Graphs** §10

a $y = -f(x)$ is $y = f(x)$ reflected in the y-axis.

b $y = 2f(-x)$ is $y = f(-x)$ scaled by 2 in the y-direction.

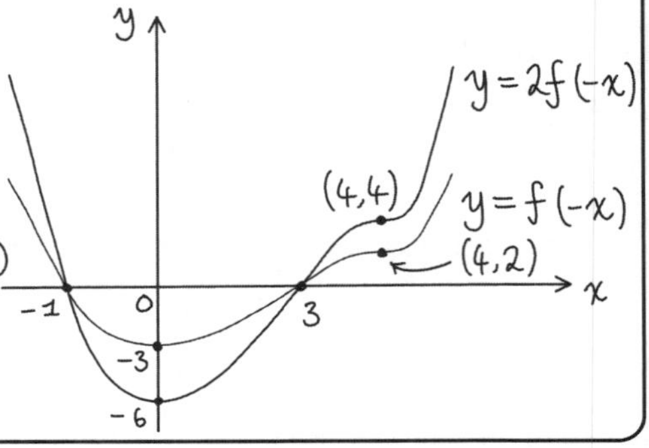

6

See **Further Calculus** §4

$$f'(x) = -2\sin 2x - 12\cos 4x$$

$$f'\left(\tfrac{\pi}{6}\right) = -2\sin\frac{2\pi}{6} - 12\cos\frac{4\pi}{6}$$

$$= -2\sin\frac{\pi}{3} - 12\cos\frac{2\pi}{3}$$

$$= -2\frac{\sqrt{3}}{2} + 12 \times \frac{1}{2}$$

$$= 6 - \sqrt{3}.$$

Using:

- $\frac{d}{dx}(\sin ax) = a\cos ax.$
- $\frac{d}{dx}(\cos ax) = -a\sin ax.$

Exact values...

$$\cos\frac{2\pi}{3} = -\cos\frac{\pi}{3}$$

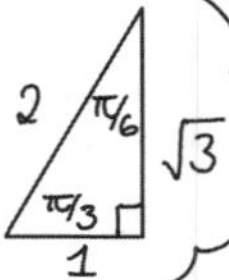

7

See **Wave Functions** §2 and §4

a)
$$2\sin x° + 5\cos x° = k\sin(x° + a°)$$
$$= k\sin x° \cos a° + k\cos x° \sin a°$$
$$= (k\cos a°)\sin x° + (k\sin a°)\cos x°.$$

Comparing coefficients:
$$k\sin a° = 5$$
$$k\cos a° = 2$$

$$\begin{array}{c|c} \checkmark_S & A^{\checkmark\checkmark} \\ \hline T & C^\checkmark \end{array}$$

So $k = \sqrt{5^2 + 2^2}$ and $\tan a° = \dfrac{k\sin a°}{k\cos a°} = \dfrac{5}{2}$
$$= \sqrt{25 + 4}$$
$$= \sqrt{29}$$

$$a = \tan^{-1}\left(\frac{5}{2}\right) = 68\cdot20 \quad (\text{to 2 d.p.})$$

So $2\sin x° + 5\cos x° = \sqrt{29}\sin(x° + 68\cdot20°).$

b) The minimum occurs when
$$\sin(x° + 68\cdot20°) = -1$$
$$x + 68\cdot20 = 270$$
$$x = 270 - 201\cdot80$$
$$= 201\cdot80$$

So P is $(201\cdot80, -\sqrt{29})$.

The curve goes up to $\sqrt{29}$ and down to $-\sqrt{29}$.

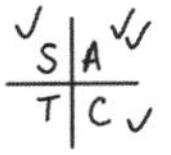

8

See **Differentiation** §12

a 108 litres = 108 000 cm^3.

The volume is $\frac{1}{2}x^2 l = 108\,000$ so $l = \frac{216\,000}{x^2}$.

The surface area is
$$A(x) = x^2 + 2xl$$
$$= x^2 + 2x\frac{216\,000}{x^2}$$
$$= x^2 + \frac{432\,000}{x}.$$

b Stationary values exist when $A'(x) = 0$.

$$A(x) = x^2 + 432000x^{-1}.$$
$$A'(x) = 2x - \frac{432\,000}{x^2} = 0$$
$$2x^3 = 432000$$
$$x^3 = 216\,000$$
$$x = 60.$$

Check this gives a minimum...

x	60^-	60	60^+
$A'(x)$	$-$	0	$+$
Sketch	\	_	/

So the minimum area occurs when $x = 60$.

9

See **Vectors** §14

$$\underline{a}.(\underline{a}+\underline{b}) = \underline{a}.\underline{a} + \underline{a}.\underline{b}$$
$$= |\underline{a}|^2 + |\underline{a}||\underline{b}|\cos\theta$$
$$36 = 5^2 + 5\times 4\cos\theta$$
$$20\cos\theta = 11$$
$$\cos\theta = \frac{11}{20}$$
$$\theta = \cos^{-1}\left(\frac{11}{20}\right)$$
$$= 56{\cdot}63^\circ \text{ (to 2 d.p.)}$$
or $0{\cdot}988$ radians (to 3 d.p.)

Remember: $\underline{u}.\underline{u} = |\underline{u}|^2$

10

See **Trigonometry** §5

$$3\cos 2x + 10\cos x - 1 = 0$$
$$3(2\cos^2 x - 1) + 10\cos x - 1 = 0$$
$$6\cos^2 x - 3 + 10\cos x - 1 = 0$$
$$6\cos^2 x + 10\cos x - 4 = 0$$
$$3\cos^2 x + 5\cos x - 2 = 0$$
$$(3\cos x - 1)(\cos x + 2) = 0$$

$3\cos x = 1$ or $\cos x = -2$

$\cos x = \frac{1}{3}$ (S | A ✓ / T | C ← Not here since $0 \leq x \leq \pi$.)

No solutions since $-1 \leq \cos x \leq 1$.

$$x = \cos^{-1}\left(\frac{1}{3}\right)$$
$$= 1.23 \text{ radians (to 2 d.p.)}$$

11

(a) See **Functions and Graphs** §5 and §10
(b) See **Exponentials and Logarithms** §5

a i $y = a^x$ passes through $(0,1)$ and $(1,a)$.

So $y = a^x + 1$ passes through $(0,2)$ and $(1,a+1)$

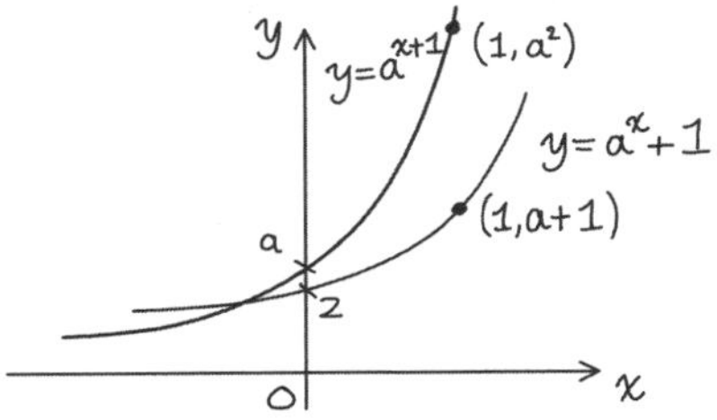

ii $y = a^{x+1}$ is $y = a^x$ shifted 1 place to the left.

When $x = 0$, $y = a^1 = a$. $(0, a)$

When $x = 1$, $y = a^2$. $(1, a^2)$.

b At points of intersection

$$a^{x+1} = a^x + 1$$
$$a^{x+1} - a^x = 1$$
$$a^x(a-1) = 1$$
$$a^x = \frac{1}{a-1}$$
$$x = \log_a\left(\frac{1}{a-1}\right)$$

Remember: $a^x = y \Leftrightarrow x = \log_a y$

2004 Paper 1

1

See **Straight Lines** – (a) §10 and §3, (b) §6 and §5

a Point of intersection...

$$x + 3y + 1 = 0 \quad \text{——} \; ①$$
$$2x + 5y = 0 \quad \text{——} \; ②$$

$2 \times ①$: $2x + 6y + 2 = 0$ —— ③

③ − ②: $y + 2 = 0$

$y = -2.$

When $y = -2$, ② becomes $2x - 10 = 0$

$x = 5.$ So $B(5, -2)$.

So $m_{AB} = \dfrac{-2-4}{5-7} = \dfrac{-6}{-2} = 3.$

b $x + 3y + 1 = 0$

$3y = -x - 1$

$y = -\frac{1}{3}x - \frac{1}{3}.$

Remember:
To extract the gradient, rearrange to the form $y = mx + c$.

So the gradient is $m_1 = -\frac{1}{3}$.

This line is perpendicular to AB since $m_1 \times m_{AB} = -1$.

$2x + 5y = 0$

$5y = -2x$

$y = -\frac{2}{5}x.$ So the gradient is $m_2 = -\frac{2}{5}$.

This line is not perpendicular to AB since:

$$m_2 \times m_{AB} = -\frac{2}{5} \times 3 = -\frac{6}{5} \neq -1.$$

2

See **Polynomials and Quadratics** – (a) §9, (b) §12

a **i** Evaluate $f(-1)$...

$$-1 \begin{array}{|rrrr} 1 & -1 & -5 & -3 \\ & -1 & 2 & 3 \\ \hline 1 & -2 & -3 & \boxed{0} \end{array}$$

or

$$f(-1) = (-1)^3 - (-1)^2 - 5(-1) - 3$$
$$= -1 - 1 + 5 - 3$$
$$= 0.$$

Since $f(-1) = 0$, $(x+1)$ is a factor.

ii $f(x) = (x+1)(x^2 - 2x - 3)$
$\quad\quad = (x+1)(x+1)(x-3)$

Either from the bottom row of the table or by inspection.

b Since there is a repeated factor of $(x+1)$, there is a turning point at $(-1, 0)$.

3

See **Trigonometry** §1

$\tan^2 x = 3$

$\tan x = \pm\sqrt{3}$

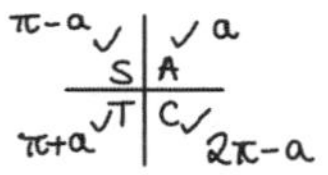

$$\begin{array}{c|c} \pi - a \;\checkmark\; S & A \;\checkmark\; a \\ \hline \pi + a \;\checkmark\; T & C \;\checkmark\; 2\pi - a \end{array}$$

$a = \tan^{-1}(\sqrt{3})$
$\quad = \dfrac{\pi}{3}.$

Remember:
$\tan^2 x \equiv (\tan x)^2.$

Exact value...

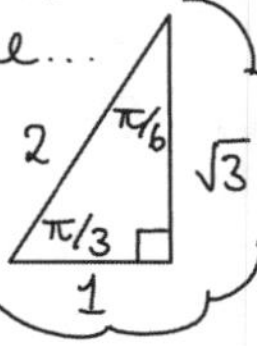

So $x = \dfrac{\pi}{3}$ or $\pi - \dfrac{\pi}{3}$ or $\pi + \dfrac{\pi}{3}$ or $2\pi - \dfrac{\pi}{3}.$

$\quad = \dfrac{\pi}{3}$ or $\dfrac{2\pi}{3}$ or $\dfrac{4\pi}{3}$ or $\dfrac{5\pi}{3}.$

4

See **Functions and Graphs** §10

a $y = -g(x)$ is $y = g(x)$ reflected in the x-axis.

b $3 - g(x) = -g(x) + 3$.

So $y = 3 - g(x)$ is $y = -g(x)$ shifted up by 3.

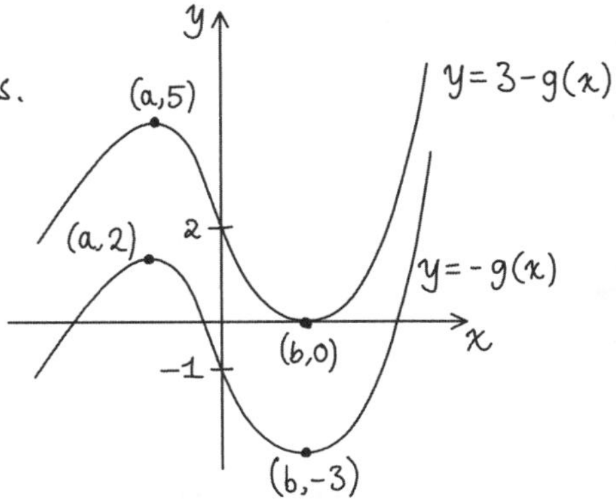

5

See **Vectors** – (a) §9, (b) §10

a
$$\vec{AB} = \underline{b} - \underline{a} = \begin{pmatrix} -1 \\ 8 \\ 3 \end{pmatrix} - \begin{pmatrix} -3 \\ 4 \\ 7 \end{pmatrix} = \begin{pmatrix} 2 \\ 4 \\ -4 \end{pmatrix}$$

$$\vec{BC} = \underline{c} - \underline{b} = \begin{pmatrix} 0 \\ 10 \\ 1 \end{pmatrix} - \begin{pmatrix} -1 \\ 8 \\ 3 \end{pmatrix} = \begin{pmatrix} 1 \\ 2 \\ -2 \end{pmatrix} = \frac{1}{2}\vec{AB}$$

Since these have the same direction (i.e. they are multiples of the same vector) and B is a common point, the points A, B and C are collinear.

b
$$\vec{AD} = 4\vec{AB}$$

$$\underline{d} - \underline{a} = 4(\underline{b} - \underline{a})$$

$$\underline{d} = 4\underline{b} - 4\underline{a} + \underline{a}$$

$$= 4\underline{b} - 3\underline{a}$$

$$= 4\begin{pmatrix} -1 \\ 8 \\ 3 \end{pmatrix} - 3\begin{pmatrix} -3 \\ 4 \\ 7 \end{pmatrix}$$

$$= \begin{pmatrix} -4 \\ 32 \\ 12 \end{pmatrix} - \begin{pmatrix} -9 \\ 12 \\ 21 \end{pmatrix}$$

$$= \begin{pmatrix} 5 \\ 20 \\ -9 \end{pmatrix}.$$ So D has coordinates $(5, 20, -9)$.

6

See **Further Calculus** §4

$$y = 3\sin x + \cos 2x$$
$$\frac{dy}{dx} = 3\cos x - 2\sin 2x$$

Using:
$$\frac{d}{dx}(\cos ax) = -a\sin ax$$

7

See **Further Calculus** §5

$$\int_0^2 \sqrt{4x+1}\,dx = \int_0^2 (4x+1)^{1/2}\,dx$$
$$= \left[\frac{(4x+1)^{3/2}}{\frac{3}{2}\times 4}\right]_0^2$$
$$= \left[\frac{1}{6}\sqrt{4x+1}^{\,3}\right]_0^2$$
$$= \frac{1}{6}\sqrt{9}^{\,3} - \frac{1}{6}\sqrt{1}^{\,3}$$
$$= \frac{3^3}{6} - \frac{1}{6}$$
$$= \frac{26}{6}$$
$$= \frac{13}{3}.$$

Remember:
$$\int (ax+b)^n\,dx = \frac{(ax+b)^{n+1}}{a(n+1)} + c$$

8

(a) See **Polynomials and Quadratics** §3
(b) See **Differentiation** §6

a <u>Method 1</u> Compensating...

$$x^2 - 10x + 27 = (x-5)^2 - 25 + 27 = (x-5)^2 + 2.$$

This gives the correct x^2 and x terms, and an extra 25

Take off this extra 25.

cont...

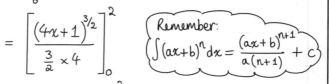

Method 2 Comparing coefficients...

$$x^2 - 10x + 27 = (x+b)^2 + c$$
$$= x^2 + 2bx + b^2 + c.$$

So $2b = -10$ and $b^2 + c = 27$

$b = -5$ $\quad c = 27 - 25$

$= 2.$

So $x^2 - 10x + 27 = (x-5)^2 + 2.$

b $g'(x) = x^2 - 10x + 27$

$= (x-5)^2 + 2$

"Increasing" means $g'(x) > 0$.

But $(x-5)^2 \geqslant 0$ for all x,

so $(x-5)^2 + 2 > 0$ for all x. Hence g is always increasing.

9

See **Exponentials and Logarithms** §5

$$\log_2(x+1) - 2\log_2 3 = 3$$
$$\log_2(x+1) - \log_2 3^2 = 3$$
$$\log_2\left(\frac{x+1}{9}\right) = 3$$
$$\frac{x+1}{9} = 2^3$$
$$x+1 = 72$$
$$x = 71.$$

Remember:

- $k\log_a x = \log_a x^k$.
- $\log_a x - \log_a y = \log_a \frac{x}{y}$.
- $y = \log_a x \Leftrightarrow x = a^y$.

10

See **Trigonometry** §3 and §4

From the diagram: $D\hat{E}A = 2x + 90$.

So $\cos(D\hat{E}A^\circ) = \cos(2x^\circ + 90^\circ)$

$= -\sin(2x^\circ)$

$= -2\sin x^\circ \cos x^\circ$

$= -2 \times \frac{1}{\sqrt{10}} \times \frac{3}{\sqrt{10}}$

$= -\frac{6}{10} = -\frac{3}{5}$.

Remember: $\cos(x^\circ + 90^\circ) = -\sin x^\circ$.

By Pythagoras's Theorem:

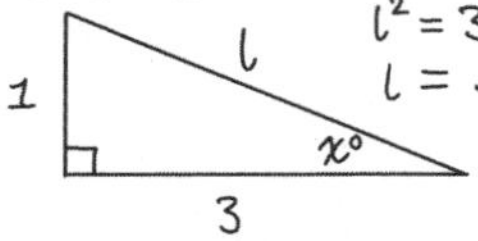

$l^2 = 3^2 + 1^2$

$l = \sqrt{10}$.

11

(a) See **Polynomials and Quadratics** §5
(b) See **Integration** §3

a The parabola crosses the x-axis at $x = 0$ and $x = 2$, so x and $(x-2)$ are factors, i.e. $b = 2$.

The point $(1, -6)$ lies on the parabola, so

$-6 = a \times 1(1-2)$

$-6 = -a$

$a = 6$.

b $f(x) = \int f'(x)\,dx$

$= \int 6x(x-2)\,dx$

$= \int (6x^2 - 12x)\,dx$

$= \frac{6x^3}{3} - \frac{12x^2}{2} + c$

$= 2x^3 - 6x^2 + c$.

We know $f(1) = 4$, i.e. $2 \times 1^3 - 6 \times 1^2 + c = 4$

$-4 + c = 4$

$c = 8$.

So $f(x) = 2x^3 - 6x^2 + 8$.

2004 Paper 2

1

See **Straight Lines** – (a) §6 and §3, (b) §3

a

$$x - 2y = 0$$
$$x = 2y$$
$$y = \frac{1}{2}x. \quad \text{So } m = \frac{1}{2}.$$

Remember:
To extract the gradient, rearrange to the form $y = mx + c$.

$$m = \tan a^\circ$$
$$\tan a^\circ = \frac{1}{2}$$
$$a^\circ = \tan^{-1}\left(\frac{1}{2}\right)$$
$$a = 26{\cdot}57 \text{ (to 2 d.p.)}$$

b

$$m_{OB} = \tan(30^\circ + a^\circ)$$
$$= \tan(30^\circ + 26{\cdot}57^\circ)$$
$$= \tan(56{\cdot}57^\circ)$$
$$= 1{\cdot}5 \text{ (to 1 d.p.)}$$

2

See **Vectors** – (a) §7, (b) §12

a

$$\overrightarrow{QP} = \underset{\sim}{p} - \underset{\sim}{q} = \begin{pmatrix} 1 \\ 3 \\ -1 \end{pmatrix} - \begin{pmatrix} 2 \\ 0 \\ 1 \end{pmatrix} = \begin{pmatrix} -1 \\ 3 \\ -2 \end{pmatrix}.$$

$$\overrightarrow{QR} = \underset{\sim}{r} - \underset{\sim}{q} = \begin{pmatrix} -3 \\ 1 \\ 2 \end{pmatrix} - \begin{pmatrix} 2 \\ 0 \\ 1 \end{pmatrix} = \begin{pmatrix} -5 \\ 1 \\ 1 \end{pmatrix}.$$

cont...

2004

b $|\overrightarrow{QP}| = \sqrt{(-1)^2 + 3^2 + (-2)^2} = \sqrt{1+9+4} = \sqrt{14}$

$|\overrightarrow{QR}| = \sqrt{(-5)^2 + 1^2 + 1^2} = \sqrt{25+1+1} = \sqrt{27}$

$\overrightarrow{QP}.\overrightarrow{QR} = -1\times(-5) + 3\times 1 - 2\times 1 = 5+3-2 = 6.$

$$\cos P\hat{Q}R = \frac{\overrightarrow{QP}.\overrightarrow{QR}}{|\overrightarrow{QP}||\overrightarrow{QR}|} = \frac{6}{\sqrt{14}\sqrt{27}}$$

Using: $\underline{a}.\underline{b} = |\underline{a}||\underline{b}|\cos\theta$

$$P\hat{Q}R = \cos^{-1}\left(\frac{6}{\sqrt{14}\sqrt{27}}\right) = 72.02^\circ \text{ (to 2 d.p.)}$$

OR 1.257 rads (to 3 d.p.)

3

See **Polynomials and Quadratics** §2

Given $2x^2 + px - 3 = 0$, let $a = 2$, $b = p$ and $c = -3$.

$$b^2 - 4ac = p^2 - 4\times 2\times(-3) = p^2 + 24.$$

But $p^2 \geq 0$ for all p, so $p^2 + 24 > 0$ for all p.

Hence the equation has real (and distinct) roots for all p.

4

See **Sequences** §4

a $-1 < k < 1$

b Method 1 $\quad l = \frac{b}{1-a}$ with $l = 5$, $a = k$ and $b = 3$.

So $5 = \frac{3}{1-k}$

$5(1-k) = 3$

$5 - 5k = 3$

$5k = 2$

$k = \frac{2}{5}.$

cont...

Method 2 As $n \to \infty$, $u_{n+1} = u_n = 5$. So $5 = 5k + 3$

$$5k = 2$$
$$k = \frac{2}{5}.$$

2004

5

See **Differentiation** §5

a

$$y = 6x^2 - x^3$$
$$\frac{dy}{dx} = 12x - 3x^2$$

Remember: $\frac{dy}{dx} = m_{tangent}$.

Since the tangent at P has gradient 12:

$$12x - 3x^2 = 12$$
$$3x^2 - 12x + 12 = 0$$
$$x^2 - 4x + 4 = 0$$
$$(x-2)^2 = 0$$
$$x = 2.$$

b When $x = 2$, $y = 6 \times 2^2 - 2^3 = 24 - 8 = 16$. So P is $(2, 16)$.

The equation of the tangent is $y - 16 = 12(x - 2)$

$$y - 16 = 12x - 24$$
$$12x - y - 8 = 0.$$

6

See **Wave Functions** §5

2004

a) $3\cos x° + 5\sin x° = k\cos(x° - a°)$

$$= k\cos x° \cos a° + k\sin x° \sin a°.$$

$$= (k\cos a°)\cos x° + (k\sin a°)\sin x°.$$

Comparing coefficients: $\quad k\sin a° = 5$ $\quad k\cos a° = 3$

$$\begin{array}{c|c} ✓ S & A ✓✓ \\ \hline T & C ✓ \end{array}$$

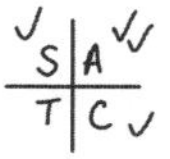

So $k = \sqrt{5^2 + 3^2}$ and $\tan a° = \dfrac{k\sin a°}{k\cos a°} = \dfrac{5}{3}$

$$= \sqrt{25+9}$$
$$= \sqrt{34}$$

$$a = \tan^{-1}\left(\frac{5}{3}\right) = 59.04 \quad \text{(to 2 d.p.)}$$

So $3\cos x° + 5\sin x° = \sqrt{34}\cos(x° - 59.04°)$.

b)
$$3\cos x° + 5\sin x° = 4 \qquad 0 \leqslant x \leqslant 90$$
$$\sqrt{34}\cos(x° - 59.04°) = 4 \qquad -59.04 \leqslant x - 59.04 \leqslant 30.96.^*$$
$$\cos(x° - 59.04°) = \frac{4}{\sqrt{34}}$$

$$\begin{array}{c|c} 180-a & ✓a \\ S & A \\ \hline T & C ✓ \\ 180+a & 360-a \end{array}$$

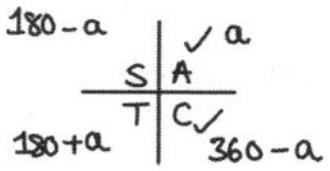

$$a = \cos^{-1}\left(\frac{4}{\sqrt{34}}\right)$$
$$= 46.69 \quad (2\,\text{d.p.})$$

$$x - 59.04 = 46.69 \text{ or } 360 - 46.69$$
$$= \cancel{46.69} \text{ or } \cancel{313.31}$$
$$\text{too large (see}^*\text{)}$$

Look 360° backwards:

$$x - 59.04 = 46.69 - 360 \text{ or } 313.31 - 360$$
$$= -\cancel{313.31} \quad \text{or} \quad -46.69$$
$$\text{too small}$$

So $\quad x = -46.69 + 59.04$

$$= 12.35.$$

7

See **Differentiation** §11

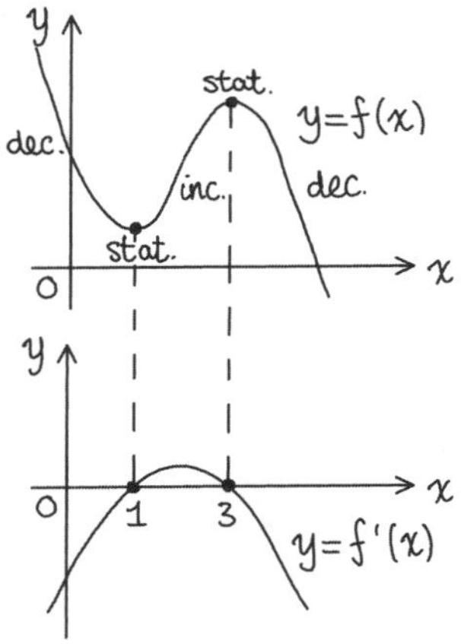

dec: f(x) is decreasing so $f'(x) < 0$, i.e. $f'(x)$ is below the x-axis.

inc: f(x) is increasing so $f'(x) > 0$, i.e. $f'(x)$ is above the x-axis.

stat: f(x) is stationary so $f'(x) = 0$, i.e. $f'(x)$ lies on the x-axis.

8

(a) See **Circles** §6 or §5
(b) See **Circles** §5
(c) See **Straight Lines** §1

a Method 1

The centre is A(6, 1).

$$m_{AP} = \frac{-1-1}{5-6} = \frac{-2}{-1} = 2.$$

Using: $x^2 + y^2 + 2gx + 2fy + c = 0$ has centre $(-g, -f)$.

So $m_{PT} = -\frac{1}{2}$ since the radius and tangent are perpendicular.

The equation of PT is:

$y + 1 = -\frac{1}{2}(x-5)$ using point P(5, −1).

$2y + 2 = -(x-5)$ multiplying by 2.

$2y + 2 = -x + 5$

$x + 2y = 3.$

cont...

2004

Method 2 Write $x+2y=3$ as $x=3-2y$ and substitute into the equation of the circle:

$$(3-2y)^2+y^2-12(3-2y)-2y+32=0$$
$$9-12y+4y^2+y^2-36+24y-2y+32=0$$
$$5y^2+10y+5=0$$
$$y^2+2y+1=0$$
$$(y+1)^2=0.$$

Since there is only one solution, the line is a tangent.
Check that P lies on the line: $x=3-2\times(-1)=5$.

b Line PT has equation $x=3-2y$. To find points of intersection, substitute this into the equation of the circle:

$$(3-2y)^2+y^2+10(3-2y)+2y+6=0$$
$$9-12y+4y^2+y^2+30-20y+2y+6=0$$
$$5y^2-30y+45=0$$
$$y^2-6y+9=0$$
$$(y-3)^2=0$$
$$y=3$$

You could also use the discriminant to show there is just one solution.

Since there is only one solution, the line is a tangent.

c When $y=3$, $x=3-2\times3=-3$. So Q is the point $(-3,3)$.

So $PQ=\sqrt{(-3-5)^2+(3-(-1))^2}$
$=\sqrt{64+16}$
$=\sqrt{80}$
$=4\sqrt{5}$

9

See **Differentiation** §12

a We are told that the surface area is 12 square units.

The surface area is given by:

$$2 \times \text{short side} + 2 \times \text{long side} + \text{base}$$
$$= 2 \times 2x \times h + 2 \times x \times h + 2x \times x$$
$$= 6xh + 2x^2 = 12$$

So
$$6xh = 12 - 2x^2$$
$$3xh = 6 - x^2$$
$$h = \frac{6-x^2}{3x}.$$

The volume is $V(x) = 2x \times x \times h = 2x^2 \cdot \frac{6-x^2}{3x} = \frac{2}{3}x(6-x^2)$.

b Stationary values exist where $V'(x) = 0$.

$$V(x) = \frac{2}{3}x(6-x^2) = 4x - \frac{2}{3}x^3.$$
$$V'(x) = 4 - 2x^2 = 0$$
$$2x^2 = 4$$
$$x^2 = 2$$
$$x = \sqrt{2}$$ (no "±" since lengths are positive)

Check this gives a maximum...

x	$\sqrt{2}^-$	$\sqrt{2}$	$\sqrt{2}^+$
$V'(x)$	+	0	−
Sketch	/	—	\

Hence the maximum volume occurs when $x = \sqrt{2}$.

2004

10

See **Exponentials and Logarithms** §5

a We are told that $A_{1000} = 600$, i.e.:

$$A_0 e^{0.002 \times 1000} = 600$$
$$A_0 e^{-2} = 600$$
$$A_0 = \frac{600}{e^{-2}}$$
$$= 600e^2$$
$$= 4433.43 \text{ micrograms (to 2 d.p.)}$$

b

$$A_t = \frac{1}{2} A_0$$
$$A_0 e^{-0.002t} = \frac{1}{2} A_0$$
$$e^{-0.002t} = \frac{1}{2}$$
$$\log_e e^{-0.002t} = \log_e \frac{1}{2} \quad \text{(taking } \log_e \text{ on both sides)}$$
$$-0.002t = \log_e \frac{1}{2}$$
$$t = -\frac{\log_e \frac{1}{2}}{0.002}$$
$$= 346.57 \text{ years (to 2 d.p.)}$$

Remember:
- $\log_a x^k = k \log_a x$
- $\log_a a = 1$.

11

See **Integration** §6

To find the limits of integration...

$$2x - \frac{1}{2}x^2 = 1{\cdot}5$$

$$4x - x^2 = 3 \qquad \text{multiplying through by 2.}$$

$$x^2 - 4x + 3 = 0$$

$$(x-1)(x-3) = 0$$

$$x = 1 \quad \text{or} \quad x = 3.$$

The shaded area is given by:

$$\int_1^3 (\text{upper} - \text{lower})\,dx = \int_1^3 \left(2x - \frac{1}{2}x^2 - 1{\cdot}5\right) dx$$

$$= \left[x^2 - \frac{1}{6}x^3 - 1{\cdot}5x\right]_1^3$$

$$= 9 - \frac{27}{6} - 4{\cdot}5 - \left(1 - \frac{1}{6} - 1{\cdot}5\right)$$

$$= \frac{2}{3} \text{ square units.}$$

2005 Paper 1

1

See **Straight Lines** §3 and §6

$m = \tan\theta$

$= \tan 60°$

$= \sqrt{3}.$

Exact value...

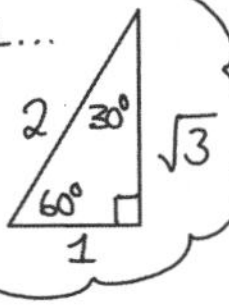

The equation of the line is

$$y - 0 = \sqrt{3}(x - (-2)) \quad \text{using point } T(-2, 0).$$

$$y = \sqrt{3}x + 2\sqrt{3}$$

$$\sqrt{3}x - y + 2\sqrt{3} = 0.$$

2

(a) See **Circles** §3 and **Straight Lines** §2
(b) See **Straight Lines** §1 or **Circles** §3

a A is $(-3,-2)$ and B is $(3,6)$

P is the midpoint of A and B...

$$\left(\frac{-3+3}{2}, \frac{-2+6}{2}\right) = (0, 2).$$

Using:
$x^2 + y^2 + 2gx + 2fy + c = 0$
has centre $(-g, -f)$.

b Method 1

$$AB = \sqrt{(3+3)^2 + (6+2)^2}$$
$$= \sqrt{36+64}$$
$$= \sqrt{100}$$
$$= 10.$$

Remember:
The distance between (x_1, y_1) and (x_2, y_2) is
$\sqrt{(x_2 - x_1)^2 + (y_2 - y_1)^2}$.

Method 2 The radius of the each circle is

$$r = \sqrt{3^2 + 2^2 + 12}$$
$$= \sqrt{9+4+12}$$
$$= \sqrt{25}$$
$$= 5.$$

Using:
$x^2 + y^2 + 2gx + 2fy + c = 0$
has radius $\sqrt{g^2 + f^2 - c}$.

So $AB = 2r = 10.$

3

See **Vectors** §10 and §7

a From the diagram:

$$\vec{OF} = \vec{OB} + \tfrac{1}{3}\vec{BD}$$
$$= \underline{b} + \tfrac{1}{3}(\underline{d} - \underline{b})$$
$$= \underline{b} + \tfrac{1}{3}\underline{d} - \tfrac{1}{3}\underline{b}$$
$$= \tfrac{2}{3}\underline{b} + \tfrac{1}{3}\underline{d}$$
$$= \tfrac{2}{3}\begin{pmatrix}12\\6\\0\end{pmatrix} + \tfrac{1}{3}\begin{pmatrix}6\\3\\9\end{pmatrix}$$
$$= \begin{pmatrix}8\\4\\0\end{pmatrix} + \begin{pmatrix}2\\1\\3\end{pmatrix}$$
$$= \begin{pmatrix}10\\5\\3\end{pmatrix}.$$

So F is $(10,5,3)$.

b $\vec{AF} = \underline{f} - \underline{a} = \begin{pmatrix}10\\5\\3\end{pmatrix} - \begin{pmatrix}12\\0\\0\end{pmatrix} = \begin{pmatrix}-2\\5\\3\end{pmatrix}.$

4

(a) See **Functions and Graphs** §3
(b) See **Polynomials and Quadratics** §3 and **Functions and Graphs** §2

a $h(x) = g(f(x)) = g(3x-1) = (3x-1)^2 + 7.$

b i The minimum occurs when $3x - 1 = 0$ i.e. $x = \frac{1}{3}$.
So $(\frac{1}{3}, 7)$ is the minimum turning point.

ii $y \geqslant 7,\ y \in \mathbb{R}$

or more formally

$\{y \in \mathbb{R} : y \geqslant 7\}$

Remember:
The range is the set of numbers which the function produces.

5

See **Further Calculus** §4 and §1

$$\frac{d}{dx}(1+2\sin x)^4 = 4(1+2\sin x)^3 \times \frac{d}{dx}(1+2\sin x)$$
$$= 4(1+2\sin x)^3 \times 2\cos x.$$
$$= 8\cos x(1+2\sin x)^3.$$

Remember the Chain Rule.

Using: $\frac{d}{dx}(\sin x) = \cos x.$

6

See **Sequences** – (a) §4, (b) §1, §2 and §3

a <u>Method 1</u> $l = \frac{b}{1-a}$ where $a = k$, $b = 5$, $l = 4$, i.e.

$$4 = \frac{5}{1-k}$$
$$4 - 4k = 5$$
$$4k = -1$$
$$k = -\frac{1}{4}.$$

<u>Method 2</u> As $n \to \infty$, $u_{n+1} = u_n = 4$.

$$4 = 4k + 5$$
$$4k = -1$$
$$k = -\frac{1}{4}.$$

b i $u_1 = mu_0 + 5 = 3m + 5.$

$u_2 = mu_1 + 5 = m(3m+5) + 5 = 3m^2 + 5m + 5.$

ii
$$u_2 = 7$$
$$3m^2 + 5m + 5 = 7$$
$$3m^2 + 5m - 2 = 0$$
$$(3m-1)(m+2) = 0$$
$$m = \frac{1}{3} \text{ or } m = -2.$$

Since there is a limit for $-1 < m < 1$, when $m = -2$ there is no limit.

7

(a) See **Functions and Graphs** *§6 and* **Exponentials and Logarithms** *§2*
(a) See **Functions and Graphs** *§2*

a $y = \log_b x$ passes through $(1,0)$. To get $y = f(x)$, shift 4 places to the right. So $a = 4$.

$y = \log_b(x-4)$ passes through $(9,1)$ so $\log_b(9-4) = 1$

$$\log_b 5 = 1$$
$$b = 5.$$

b $f(x)$ is only defined for $x-4>0$ i.e. $x>4$.

or more formally $\{x \in \mathbb{R} : x > 4\}$.

8

(a) and (b) See **Polynomials and Quadratics** *§9*
(c) See **Differentiation** *§10*

a Evaluate $f(3)$...

3	2	−7	0	9
		6	−3	−9
	2	−1	−3	0

(There is no x term.)

OR $f(3) = 2\times 3^3 - 7\times 3^2 + 9$
$= 2\times 27 - 7\times 9 + 9$
$= 54 - 63 + 9$
$= 0.$

Since $f(3)=0$, $(x-3)$ is a factor.

$f(x) = (x-3)(2x^2 - x - 3)$
$= (x-3)(2x-3)(x+1)$.

(Either from the bottom row of the table or by inspection.)

b Crosses the y-axis when $x=0$...

$y = 2\times 0^3 - 7\times 0^2 + 9 = 9$ $(0,9)$.

Crosses the x-axis when $y=0$...

$(x-3)(2x-3)(x+1) = 0$

$x=3$ or $x=\frac{3}{2}$ or $x=-1$.

$(3,0)$ $\left(\frac{3}{2},0\right)$ $(-1,0)$.

cont...

c Extrema occur at turning points or endpoints of the interval $-2 \leq x \leq 2$.

Stationary points exist where $f'(x) = 0$.

$$f'(x) = 6x^2 - 14x = 0$$

$$2x(3x - 7) = 0$$

$$x = 0 \quad \text{or} \quad x = \frac{7}{3}$$ ← Can't be this because $\frac{7}{3} > 2$. (i.e. outside the closed interval)

When $x = 0$, $y = 9$.

Endpoints...

When $x = -2$, $y = 2 \times (-2)^3 - 7 \times (-2)^2 + 9 = -16 - 28 + 9 = -35$.

When $x = 2$, $y = 2 \times 2^3 - 7 \times 2^2 + 9 = 16 - 28 + 9 = -3$.

So the maximum value is 9 and the minimum is -35.

2005

9

See **Trigonometry** §4 and §3

Method 1

$$\cos 2x = 1 - 2\sin^2 x$$
$$\frac{7}{25} = 1 - 2\sin^2 x$$
$$2\sin^2 x = \frac{18}{25}$$
$$\sin^2 x = \frac{9}{25}$$
$$\sin x = \pm\frac{3}{5}$$

But $\sin x > 0$ since $0 < x < \frac{\pi}{2}$, so $\sin x = \frac{3}{5}$. $\left(= \frac{\text{opp.}}{\text{hyp.}}\right)$

So $\cos x = \frac{4}{5}$.

Method 2

$$\cos 2x = 2\cos^2 x - 1$$
$$\frac{7}{25} = 2\cos^2 x - 1$$
$$2\cos^2 x = \frac{32}{25}$$
$$\cos^2 x = \frac{16}{25}$$
$$\cos x = \pm\frac{4}{5}.$$

But $\cos x > 0$ since $0 < x < \frac{\pi}{2}$, so $\cos x = \frac{4}{5}$. $\left(= \frac{\text{adj.}}{\text{hyp.}}\right)$

So $\sin x = \frac{3}{5}$.

10

See **Wave Functions** §6

a

$$\sin x - \sqrt{3}\cos x = k\sin(x - a)$$
$$= k\sin x \cos a - k\cos x \sin a$$
$$= (k\cos a)\sin x - (k\sin a)\cos x.$$

Comparing coefficients:
$$k\sin a = \sqrt{3}$$
$$k\cos a = 1$$

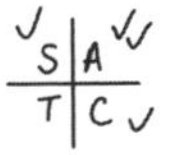

$$\begin{array}{c|c} \checkmark S & A \checkmark\checkmark \\ \hline T & C \checkmark \end{array}$$

So $k = \sqrt{\sqrt{3}^2 + 1^2}$ and $\tan a = \dfrac{k\sin a}{k\cos a} = \sqrt{3}$
$$= \sqrt{3 + 1}$$
$$= 2 \qquad\qquad a = \tan^{-1}(\sqrt{3}) = \dfrac{\pi}{3}.$$

So $\sin x - \sqrt{3}\cos x = 2\sin\left(x - \dfrac{\pi}{3}\right).$

Exact value...

b

$$y = 3 + \sin x - \sqrt{3}\cos x$$
$$= 2\sin\left(x - \dfrac{\pi}{3}\right) + 3.$$

This is the graph of $y = 2\sin\left(x - \dfrac{\pi}{3}\right)$ shifted up by 3.

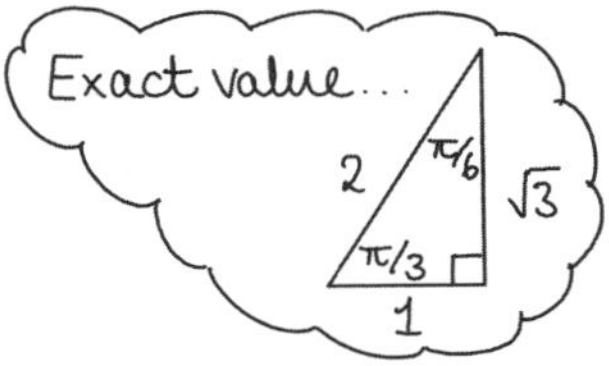

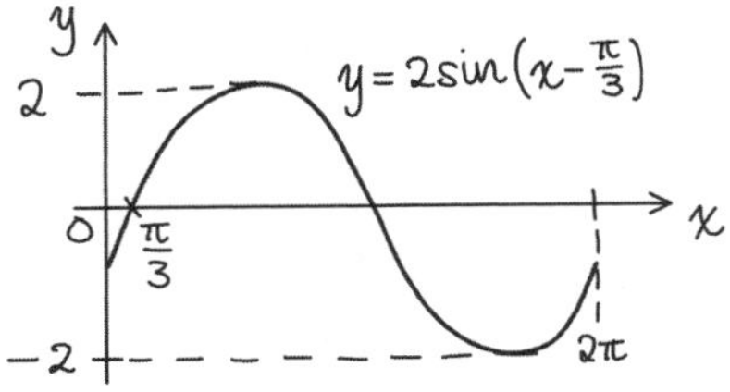

When $x = 0$, $y = 2\sin\left(-\dfrac{\pi}{3}\right) + 3$
$$= -2\sin\left(\dfrac{\pi}{3}\right) + 3$$
$$= -2 \times \dfrac{\sqrt{3}}{2} + 3$$
$$= 3 - \sqrt{3}.$$

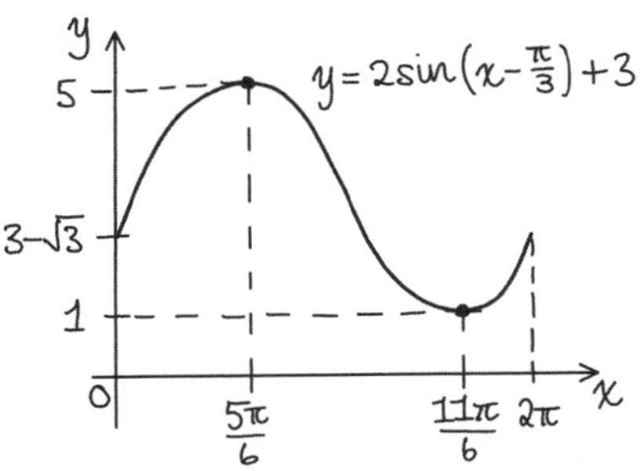

Max. and min. are moved $\dfrac{\pi}{3}$ to the right:

Max. at $x = \dfrac{\pi}{2} + \dfrac{\pi}{3} = \dfrac{5\pi}{6}.$

Min. at $x = \dfrac{3\pi}{2} + \dfrac{\pi}{3} = \dfrac{11\pi}{6}.$

2005

11

(a) See **Circles** §1
(b) See **Circles** §5 or **Straight Lines** §3

a $(x-t)^2+(y-0)^2=2^2$

$(x-t)^2+y^2=4.$

b **Method 1** Put $y=2x$ in the equation of the circle...

$$(x-t)^2+(2x)^2=4$$
$$x^2-2tx+t^2+4x^2=4$$
$$5x^2-2tx+t^2-4=0.$$

For the line to be a tangent there must be only one point of intersection, i.e. $b^2-4ac=0$ where $a=5$, $b=-2t$, $c=t^2-4$

$$(-2t)^2-4\times5(t^2-4)=0$$
$$4t^2-20t^2+80=0$$
$$-16t^2+80=0$$
$$-t^2+5=0$$
$$t=\sqrt{5} \quad \text{since } t>0.$$

Method 2 The line $y=2x$ has gradient 2.

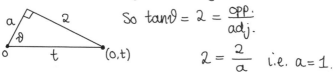

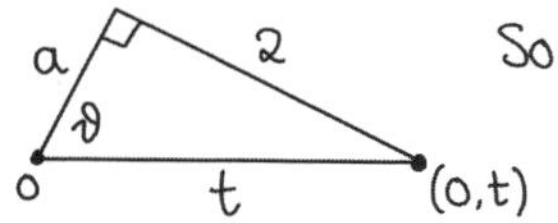

So $\tan\theta = 2 = \frac{\text{opp.}}{\text{adj.}}$

$2=\frac{2}{a}$ i.e. $a=1$.

Then using Pythagoras's Theorem $t=\sqrt{2^2+1^2}=\sqrt{5}.$

2005 Paper 2

1

See **Integration** §2

$$\frac{4x^3-1}{x^2} = \frac{4x^3}{x^2} - \frac{1}{x^2} = 4x - x^{-2}.$$

$$\text{So} \int \frac{4x^3-1}{x^2}\,dx = \int (4x - x^{-2})\,dx$$

$$= \frac{4x^2}{2} - \frac{x^{-1}}{-1} + c$$

$$= 2x^2 + \frac{1}{x} + c.$$

2

See **Trigonometry** §3

a $\sin(p+q) = \sin p \cos q + \cos p \sin q$

$$= \frac{15}{17} \times \frac{4}{5} + \frac{8}{17} \times \frac{3}{5}$$

$$= \frac{60}{85} + \frac{24}{85}$$

$$= \frac{84}{85}$$

From the diagram:

$$\sin p = \frac{15}{17} \quad \cos p = \frac{8}{17}$$

$$\sin q = \frac{6}{10} = \frac{3}{5} \quad \cos q = \frac{8}{10} = \frac{4}{5}$$

b i $\cos(p+q) = \cos p \cos q - \sin p \sin q$

$$= \frac{8}{17} \times \frac{4}{5} - \frac{15}{17} \times \frac{3}{5}$$

$$= \frac{32}{85} - \frac{45}{85}$$

$$= -\frac{13}{85}$$

ii $\tan(p+q) = \dfrac{\sin(p+q)}{\cos(p+q)} = \dfrac{\frac{84}{85}}{-\frac{13}{85}} = -\dfrac{84}{13}.$

Remember: $\tan a = \dfrac{\sin a}{\cos a}$.

2005

3

(a) See **Straight Lines** *§9*
(b) See **Circles** *§6*
(c) See **Straight Lines** *§10 and* **Circles** *§1*

a $\text{midpoint}_{AB} = \left(\frac{1+5}{2}, \frac{0+4}{2}\right) = (3, 2)$.

$m_{AB} = \frac{4-0}{5-1} = \frac{4}{4} = 1$. So $m_\perp = -1$ since $m_{AB} \times m_\perp = -1$.

The equation is $y - 2 = -1(x-3)$

$y - 2 = -x + 3$

$x + y = 5$.

b $x + 3y = 1$

$3y = -x + 1$

$y = -\frac{1}{3}x + \frac{1}{3}$

Remember:
To extract the gradient, rearrange to the form $y = mx + c$.

$m_{tangent} = -\frac{1}{3}$ so $m_{AC} = 3$ since the radius and tangent are perpendicular.

The equation is $y - 0 = 3(x-1)$ using $A(1,0)$.

$y = 3x - 3$

$3x - y = 3$.

c i The centre is the point of intersection of the perpendicular bisector of the chord and the radius.

$x + y = 5$ —— ①

$3x - y = 3$ —— ②

①+②: $4x = 8$

$x = 2$. When $x=2$, $y = 5 - 2 = 3$ (using ①).

So C is $(2,3)$.

ii The radius is $AC = \sqrt{(2-1)^2 + (3-0)^2} = \sqrt{1+9} = \sqrt{10}$ units

The equation is

$(x-2)^2 + (y-3)^2 = 10$.

The circle with centre (a, b) and radius r has equation:
$(x-a)^2 + (y-b)^2 = r^2$.

4

See **Vectors** (a) §7, (b) §12

a

$$\vec{TA} = \underline{a} - \underline{t} = \begin{pmatrix} 23 \\ 0 \\ 8 \end{pmatrix} - \begin{pmatrix} 28 \\ -15 \\ 7 \end{pmatrix} = \begin{pmatrix} -5 \\ 15 \\ 1 \end{pmatrix}.$$

$$\vec{TB} = \underline{b} - \underline{t} = \begin{pmatrix} -12 \\ 0 \\ 9 \end{pmatrix} - \begin{pmatrix} 28 \\ -15 \\ 7 \end{pmatrix} = \begin{pmatrix} -40 \\ 15 \\ 2 \end{pmatrix}.$$

b

$$|\vec{TA}| = \sqrt{(-5)^2 + 15^2 + 1^2} = \sqrt{251}.$$

$$|\vec{TB}| = \sqrt{(-40)^2 + 15^2 + 2^2} = \sqrt{1829}.$$

$$\vec{TA}.\vec{TB} = -5 \times (-40) + 15 \times 15 + 1 \times 2 = 427.$$

$$\cos A\hat{T}B = \frac{\vec{TA}.\vec{TB}}{|\vec{TA}||\vec{TB}|}$$

$$= \frac{427}{\sqrt{251}\sqrt{1829}}$$

Using: $\underline{a} . \underline{b} = |\underline{a}||\underline{b}| \cos\theta$

$$A\hat{T}B = \cos^{-1}\left(\frac{427}{\sqrt{251}\sqrt{1829}}\right)$$

$$= 50{\cdot}93^\circ \text{ (to 2 d.p.)}$$

OR $0{\cdot}889$ rads (to 3 d.p.)

5

See **Integration** §6

Points of intersection...

$$2x^2 - 9 = x^2$$
$$x^2 = 9$$
$$x = \pm 3.$$

Method 1 The area is:

$$\int_{-3}^{3} (\text{upper} - \text{lower})\,dx = \int_{-3}^{3} \left(x^2 - (2x^2 - 9)\right) dx$$
$$= \int_{-3}^{3} (-x^2 + 9)\,dx$$
$$= \left[-\tfrac{1}{3}x^3 + 9x\right]_{-3}^{3}$$
$$= (-9 + 27) - (9 - 27)$$
$$= 36 \text{ square units.}$$

Method 2 The curves are symmetrical about the y-axis, so the area is:

$$2\int_{0}^{3} (-x^2 + 9)\,dx = 2\left[-\tfrac{1}{3}x^3 + 9x\right]_{0}^{3}$$
$$= 2 \times (-9 + 27)$$
$$= 36 \text{ square units.}$$

6

See **Differentiation** §5

$y = 24x^{-1/2}$

$\frac{dy}{dx} = -12x^{-3/2} = -\frac{12}{\sqrt{x^3}}$.

When $x = 4$, $y = \frac{24}{\sqrt{4}} = 12$. So P is $(4, 12)$.

$m_{tangent} = -\frac{12}{\sqrt{4^3}} = -\frac{12}{8} = -\frac{3}{2}$.

The equation is $y - 12 = -\frac{3}{2}(x-4)$

$2y - 24 = -3x + 12$

$3x + 2y - 36 = 0$.

Remember:
$\frac{dy}{dx} = m_{tangent}$.

7

See **Exponentials and Logarithms** §5

$\log_4(5-x) - \log_4(3-x) = 2$

$\log_4\left(\frac{5-x}{3-x}\right) = 2$

$\frac{5-x}{3-x} = 4^2$

$5 - x = 16(3-x)$

$5 - x = 48 - 16x$

$15x = 43$

$x = \frac{43}{15}$.

Remember:
- $\log_a \frac{x}{y} = \log_a x - \log_a y$
- $a^x = y \Leftrightarrow x = \log_a y$

8

See **Trigonometry** §5

At points of intersection...

Using: $\sin 2A = 2\sin A\cos A$.

$$k\sin 2x = \sin x$$
$$2k\sin x\cos x = \sin x$$
$$\sin x(2k\cos x - 1) = 0$$
$$\sin x = 0 \quad \text{or} \quad 2k\cos x - 1 = 0$$
$$\cos x = \frac{1}{2k}.$$

From the diagram, $\sin x \neq 0$ at A and C, so $\cos x = \frac{1}{2k}$.

9

See **Exponentials and Logarithms** §5

a When $t=0$, $V = 252e^0 = 252$ million pounds.

b It will be sold when $V = 20$...

$$V = 20$$
$$252e^{-0.06335t} = 20$$
$$e^{-0.06335t} = \frac{20}{252}$$
$$-0.06335t = \log_e\left(\frac{20}{252}\right)$$
$$t = 39.995 \text{ (to 3 d.p.)}$$
$$= 40 \text{ years (to the nearest year)}$$

10

See **Vectors** §14

Expanding the brackets...

$$\underline{a}.(\underline{a}+\underline{b}+\underline{c}) = \underline{a}.\underline{a} + \underline{a}.\underline{b} + \underline{a}.\underline{c}$$
$$= |\underline{a}|^2 + 0 + |\underline{a}||\underline{c}|\cos\theta$$
$$= 3^2 + 3\times 3\times \cos 60^\circ$$
since the triangle is equilateral
$$= 9 + 9\times\tfrac{1}{2}$$
$$= \frac{27}{2}.$$

Remember
- $\underline{a}.\underline{b} = 0 \Leftrightarrow \underline{a}$ and $\underline{b}$ are perp.
- $\underline{a}.\underline{a} = |\underline{a}|^2$.

11

See **Polynomials and Quadratics** – (a) §9, (b) §2 and §6

a Evaluate the LHS for $x=-1$...

-1	1	p	p	1
		-1	$1-p$	-1
	1	$p-1$	1	0

OR

$$(-1)^3 + p\times(-1)^2 + p\times(-1) + 1$$
$$= -1 + p - p + 1$$
$$= 0.$$

This evaluates to the RHS, so $x=-1$ is a solution.

b
$$x^3 + px^2 + px + 1 = 0$$
$$(x+1)(x^2 + (p-1)x + 1) = 0.$$

Either from the bottom row of the table or by inspection.

Since $x=-1$ is a real root for all p, we need the roots of $x^2 + (p-1)x + 1 = 0$ to be real also.

For real roots, $b^2 - 4ac \geqslant 0$ where $a=1, b=p-1, c=1$.

$$(p-1)^2 - 4\times 1\times 1 \geqslant 0$$
$$p^2 - 2p + 1 - 4 \geqslant 0$$
$$p^2 - 2p - 3 \geqslant 0$$
$$(p-3)(p+1) \geqslant 0$$

Sketch

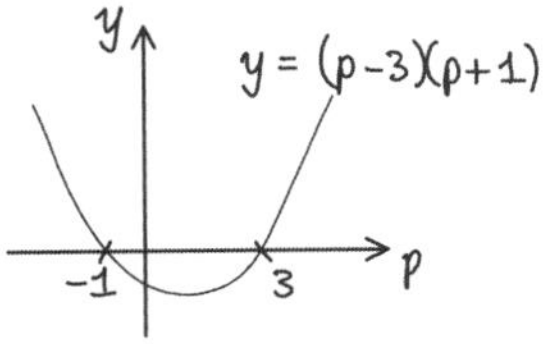

From the sketch, $p \leqslant -1$ or $p \geqslant 3$.

2006 Paper 1

1

See **Straight Lines** – (a) §7, (b) §8, (c) §10

a $D = \text{midpoint}_{AC} = \left(\frac{-1+7}{2}, \frac{12-2}{2}\right) = (3, 5).$

$m_{BD} = \frac{5-(-5)}{3-(-2)} = \frac{10}{5} = 2.$

So the equation is $y - 5 = 2(x-3)$

$$y - 5 = 2x - 6$$

$$2x - y - 1 = 0.$$

b $m_{BC} = \frac{-2-(-5)}{7-(-2)} = \frac{3}{9} = \frac{1}{3}$. So $m_{AE} = -3$ since $AE \perp BC$.

The equation is $y - 12 = -3(x-(-1))$

$$y - 12 = -3x - 3$$

$$3x + y - 9 = 0.$$

c Solve simultaneously...

$$2x - y = 1 \quad \text{——} \quad ①$$

$$3x + y = 9 \quad \text{——} \quad ②$$

①+②: $5x = 10$

$$x = 2.$$

When $x = 2$, $y = 2\times2 - 1 = 3$ (using ①).

So the point of intersection is $(2, 3)$.

2006

2

(a) See **Circles** *§1*
(b) See **Circles** *§6 and* **Straight Lines** *§2*

a $\text{Radius}^2 = CP^2 = (1-(-2))^2 + (6-3)^2 = 9+9 = 18.$

The equation of the circle is

$$(x+2)^2 + (y-3)^2 = 18.$$

The circle with centre (a, b) and radius r has equation: $(x-a)^2 + (y-b)^2 = r^2$.

b $m_{CP} = \dfrac{6-3}{1-(-2)} = \dfrac{3}{3} = 1.$

So $m_{tgt.} = -1$ since the radius and tangent are perpendicular.

Let Q be the point (x, y). Since C is the midpoint of QP

$$(-2, 3) = \left(\frac{x+1}{2}, \frac{y+6}{2}\right)$$

i.e. $\dfrac{x+1}{2} = -2$ and $\dfrac{y+6}{2} = 3$

$x+1 = -4$ $\quad$ $y+6 = 6$

$x = -5$ $\quad$ $y = 0.$

So Q is the point $(-5, 0)$.

The equation of the tangent is

$$y - 0 = -1(x - (-5))$$

$$y = -x - 5$$

$$x + y + 5 = 0.$$

3

(a) See **Functions and Graphs** *§3*
(b) See **Polynomials and Quadratics** *§3*

a i $f(g(x)) = f(2x-3) = 2(2x-3)+3 = 4x-6+3 = 4x-3$

ii $g(f(x)) = g(2x+3) = 2(2x+3)-3 = 4x+6-3 = 4x+3.$

b $f(g(x)) \times g(f(x)) = (4x-3)(4x+3) = 16x^2 - 9$

The least possible value occurs when $x = 0$, so this value is -9.

2006

4

See **Sequences** §4

a $-1 < 0.8 < 1$

b Method 1 $\quad l = \dfrac{b}{1-a}$ where $a = 0.8$ and $b = 12$.

$$l = \frac{12}{1-0.8} = \frac{12}{0.2} = \frac{120}{2} = 60.$$

Method 2 $\quad$ As $n \to \infty$, $u_{n+1} = u_n = l$.

$$l = 0.8l + 12$$
$$0.2l = 12$$
$$l = \frac{12}{0.2}$$
$$= 60.$$

5

See **Differentiation** §8 and **Further Calculus** §4

Stationary points exist where $f'(x) = 0$.

$$f'(x) = 5(2x-1)^4 \times 2 = 10(2x-1)^4.$$

Remember the Chain Rule

So
$$10(2x-1)^4 = 0$$
$$(2x-1)^4 = 0$$
$$2x - 1 = 0$$
$$x = \frac{1}{2}.$$

When $x = \frac{1}{2}$, $y = f(\frac{1}{2}) = (1-1)^5 = 0$.

So the stationary point is $(\frac{1}{2}, 0)$.

Nature:

x	$\frac{1}{2}^-$	$\frac{1}{2}$	$\frac{1}{2}^+$
$f'(x)$	+	0	+
Sketch	/	—	/

So $(\frac{1}{2}, 0)$ is a rising point of inflection.

6

See **Integration** §5

a The area S is

$$\int_0^1 (x^3-6x^2+4x+1)\,dx = \left[\tfrac{1}{4}x^4 - 2x^3 + 2x^2 + x\right]_0^1$$

$$= \tfrac{1}{4} - 2 + 2 + 1$$

$$= \tfrac{5}{4} \text{ square units.}$$

b The second area is

$$-\int_1^2 (x^3-6x^2+4x+1)\,dx = -\left[\tfrac{1}{4}x^4 - 2x^3 + 2x^2 + x\right]_1^2$$

$$= -\left(\tfrac{16}{4} - 16 + 8 + 2 - \tfrac{5}{4}\right)$$

$$= -4 + 6 + \tfrac{5}{4}$$

$$= \tfrac{13}{4} \text{ square units.}$$

(Since the area is below the x-axis.)

($\tfrac{5}{4}$ from part (a))

So the total shaded area is $\frac{13}{4} + \frac{5}{4} = \frac{18}{4} = \frac{9}{2}$ square units.

7

See **Trigonometry** §5

$$\sin x^\circ - \sin 2x^\circ = 0$$

$$\sin x^\circ - 2\sin x^\circ \cos x^\circ = 0$$

$$\sin x^\circ(1 - 2\cos x^\circ) = 0$$

(Using: $\sin 2A = 2\sin A \cos A$)

$\sin x^\circ = 0$ or $1 - 2\cos x^\circ = 0$

$x = 0, 180, 360$

$\cos x^\circ = \frac{1}{2}$

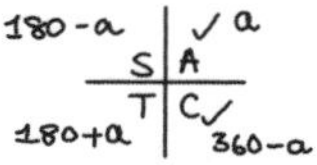

$a = \cos^{-1}\left(\frac{1}{2}\right)$

$= 60$

$x = 60$ or $360 - 60$

$= 60$ or 300

Exact value...

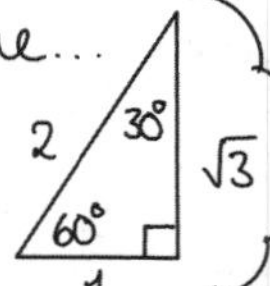

So $x = 0, 60, 180, 300, 360.$

2006

8

See **Polynomials and Quadratics** §3

a Method 1 Compensating...

$$2x^2+4x-3 = 2(x^2+2x)-3$$
$$= 2(x+1)^2-2-3 = 2(x+1)^2-5$$

This gives the correct x^2 and x terms, and an extra 2

Take off this extra 2.

Method 2 Comparing coefficients...

$$2x^2+4x-3 = a(x+b)^2+c$$
$$= ax^2+2abx+ab^2+c.$$

So $a=2$, $2ab=4$ and $ab^2+c=-3$

$b = \frac{4}{2a}$ $c = -3-ab^2$

$= 1$ $= -5.$

So $2x^2+4x-3 = 2(x+1)^2-5.$

b The turning point is $(-1,-5)$.

Remember: The parabola $y=(x-p)^2+q$ has turning point (p, q).

9

(a) See ***Vectors*** *§11*
(b) and (c) See ***Polynomials and Quadratics*** *§9*
(d) See ***Vectors*** *§12*

a $\underline{u}.\underline{v} = k^3 \times 1 + 1 \times 3k^2 - 1(k+2)$

$= k^3 + 3k^2 - k - 2.$

So $k^3 + 3k^2 - k - 2 = 1$

$k^3 + 3k^2 - k - 3 = 0.$

b Evaluate the expression for $k = -3$...

-3	1	3	-1	-3
		-3	0	3
	1	0	-1	0

or

$(-3)^3 + 3 \times (-3)^2 - (-3) - 3$

$= -27 + 27 + 3 - 3$

$= 0.$

Since the value is zero, $(k+3)$ is a factor.

So $k^3 + 3k^2 - k - 3 = (k+3)(k^2 - 1)$

$= (k+3)(k+1)(k-1)$

Either from the bottom row of the table or by inspection

c We have $k^3 + 3k^2 - k - 3 = 0$

$(k+3)(k+1)(k-1) = 0$

$k = -3, -1$ or 1.

From the question, $k > 0$ so $k = 1$.

d $|\underline{u}| = \sqrt{1^2 + 1^2 + 3^2} = \sqrt{11}$, $|\underline{v}| = \sqrt{1^2 + 3^2 + (-1)^2} = \sqrt{11}$.

$\underline{u}.\underline{v} = 1$ from part (a).

So $\cos\theta = \dfrac{\underline{u}.\underline{v}}{|\underline{u}||\underline{v}|} = \dfrac{1}{11}.$

Using: $\underline{a}.\underline{b} = |\underline{a}||\underline{b}|\cos\theta$

2006

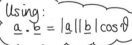

10

See **Exponentials and Logarithms** §6

<u>Method 1</u> $y = a^x$

$\log_4 y = \log_4 a^x$

We know that $\log_4 y = 3$ when $x = 6$ from the diagram, so

$3 = \log_4 a^6$

$a^6 = 4^3$

$a = 4^{3/6}$

$= 4^{1/2}$

$= 2.$

Remember: $x = \log_b y \Leftrightarrow y = b^x$.

<u>Method 2</u> The straight line has gradient $\frac{3}{6} = \frac{1}{2}$ and passes through the origin, so the equation is:

$\log_4 y = \frac{1}{2}x$

$y = 4^{\frac{x}{2}}$

$= (4^{1/2})^x$

$= 2^x.$

Just like $y = mx + c$ but with different axis labels.

Remember: $x = \log_a y \Leftrightarrow a^x = y$

So $a = 2$. (comparing to $y = a^x$).

2006

2006 Paper 2

1

See **Straight Lines** §3, §5 and §6

a $m_{PS} = \frac{6-0}{4-2} = \frac{6}{2} = 3$. So $m_{QS} = -\frac{1}{3}$ since PS and QS are perp.

The equation is $y - 6 = -\frac{1}{3}(x-4)$

$$3y - 18 = -x + 4$$

$$x + 3y = 22.$$

b Q lies on QS and the x-axis. i.e. $y=0$. So

$$x + 3\times 0 = 22$$

$x = 22$. Q is the point $(22, 0)$.

Since PQRS is a parallelogram, $\overrightarrow{PS} = \overrightarrow{QR} = \begin{pmatrix}2\\6\end{pmatrix}$.

So R is the point $(24, 6)$.

2

See **Polynomials and Quadratics** §2

For equal roots, $b^2 - 4ac = 0$ where $a = k$, $b = k$ and $c = 6$.

$$k^2 - 4\times k\times 6 = 0$$

$$k^2 - 24k = 0$$

$$k(k-24) = 0$$

~~$k=0$~~ or $k = 24$.

Question says $k \neq 0$.

So $k = 24$.

2006

3

(a) See **Differentiation** *§5*
(b) See **Polynomials and Quadratics** *§7*

a $\frac{dy}{dx} = 2x - 14.$

Remember: $\frac{dy}{dx} = m_{tangent}.$

At $x = 8$, $m_{tangent} = 2\times 8 - 14 = 2.$

So the equation is $y - 5 = 2(x - 8)$

$$y - 5 = 2x - 16$$

$$2x - y - 11 = 0. \quad (\text{or } y = 2x - 11)$$

b At points of intersection of the line and parabola:

$$2x - 11 = -x^2 + 10x - 27$$

$$x^2 - 8x + 16 = 0.$$

$$(x-4)^2 = 0$$

$$x - 4 = 0$$

$$x = 4.$$

You could also use the discriminant to show there is just one solution.

Since there is only one solution, the line is a tangent to the parabola.

Using the equation from part (a).

When $x = 4$, $y = 2\times 4 - 11 = -3$. So Q is $(4, -3)$.

4

See **Circles** *§1 and §3*

$(x-3)^2 + (y-4)^2 = 25$: centre is $(3, 4)$, radius is 5 units.

$x^2 + y^2 - kx - 8y - 2k = 0$: centre is $\left(\frac{k}{2}, 4\right)$

So $\frac{k}{2} = 3$ i.e. $k = 6$.

The radius is $\sqrt{\left(-\frac{k}{2}\right)^2 + (-4)^2 - (-2k)} = \sqrt{9 + 16 + 12} = \sqrt{37}$

Since $\sqrt{37} > 5$, the radius of the larger circle is $\sqrt{37}$ units.

2006

5

See **Integration** §3

$$y = \int \frac{dy}{dx}\,dx$$
$$= \int (4x - 6x^2)\,dx$$
$$= 2x^2 - 2x^3 + c.$$

When $x = -1$, $y = 9$ so $9 = 2\times(-1)^2 - 2\times(-1)^3 + c$

$$9 = 2 + 2 + c$$
$$c = 5.$$

So $y = 2x^2 - 2x^3 + 5.$

6

See **Vectors** §7 and §3

a $\overrightarrow{PQ} = \mathbf{q} - \mathbf{p} = \begin{pmatrix} 3 \\ 2 \\ -4 \end{pmatrix} - \begin{pmatrix} -1 \\ 2 \\ -1 \end{pmatrix} = \begin{pmatrix} 4 \\ 0 \\ -3 \end{pmatrix}.$

b $|\overrightarrow{PQ}| = \sqrt{4^2 + (-3)^2} = \sqrt{25} = 5.$

c $\frac{1}{5}\begin{pmatrix} 4 \\ 0 \\ -3 \end{pmatrix} = \begin{pmatrix} 4/5 \\ 0 \\ -3/5 \end{pmatrix}$ is a unit vector parallel to $\overrightarrow{PQ}$.

Remember: a unit vector has magnitude 1.

7

See **Functions and Graphs** §10

a $y = f(x-4)$ is $y = f(x)$ shifted 4 to the right.

b $y = 2 + f(x-4)$ is $y = f(x-4)$ shifted up 2

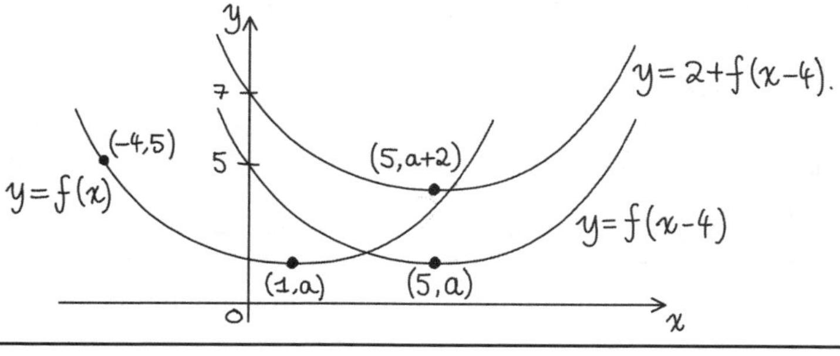

8

See **Trigonometry** §3 and §4

a i Using Pythagoras's Theorem:

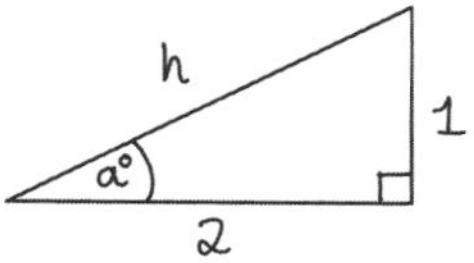

$h = \sqrt{2^2 + 1^2} = \sqrt{5}$.

$\sin a° = \frac{\text{opp.}}{\text{hyp.}} = \frac{1}{\sqrt{5}}$.

ii $\sin 2a° = 2\sin a° \cos a°$

$= 2 \times \frac{1}{\sqrt{5}} \times \frac{2}{\sqrt{5}}$

$= \frac{4}{5}$

b $\sin 3a° = \sin(2a° + a°)$

$= \sin 2a° \cos a° + \cos 2a° \sin a°$

$= \frac{4}{5} \times \frac{2}{\sqrt{5}} + \frac{3}{5} \times \frac{1}{\sqrt{5}}$

$= \frac{11}{5\sqrt{5}} \quad \left(\text{or } \frac{11\sqrt{5}}{25}\right)$

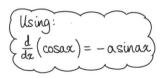

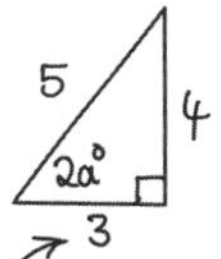

Using Pythagoras's Theorem.

2006

9

See **Further Calculus** §4

$y = x^{-3} - \cos 2x$

$\frac{dy}{dx} = -3x^{-4} + 2\sin 2x$

$= -\frac{3}{x^4} + 2\sin 2x$

Using:
$\frac{d}{dx}(\cos ax) = -a\sin ax$

10

(a) See **Wave Functions** §2
(b) See **Further Calculus** §4 and **Trigonometry** §1

a

$$7\sin x - 24\cos x = k\sin(x-a)$$
$$= k\sin x\cos a - k\cos x\sin a$$
$$= (k\cos a)\sin x - (k\sin a)\cos x$$

Comparing coefficients: $k\sin a = 24$, $k\cos a = 7$

S ✓ | A ✓✓
T | C ✓

So $k = \sqrt{7^2+24^2}$ $= \sqrt{625}$ $= 25.$ and $\tan a = \frac{k\sin a}{k\cos a} = \frac{24}{7}$

$a = \tan^{-1}\left(\frac{24}{7}\right) = 1{\cdot}287$ rads (to 3 d.p.)

So $7\sin x - 24\cos x = 25\sin(x - 1{\cdot}287)$.

b

$$\frac{dy}{dx} = 25\cos(x - 1{\cdot}287) = 1$$
$$\cos(x - 1{\cdot}287) = \frac{1}{25}$$
$$x - 1{\cdot}287 = \cos^{-1}\left(\frac{1}{25}\right)$$
$$x - 1{\cdot}287 = 1{\cdot}531$$
$$x = 2{\cdot}818 \text{ (to 3 d.p.)}$$

Remember: $\frac{dy}{dx} = m_{\text{tangent}}$.

Remember: Your calculator should be in radian mode.

11

See **Exponentials and Logarithms** §5

For 88% to be left, $A(t) = 0{\cdot}88A_0$. So:

$$0{\cdot}88A_0 = A_0 e^{-0{\cdot}000124t}$$
$$e^{-0{\cdot}000124t} = 0{\cdot}88$$
$$\log_e e^{-0{\cdot}000124t} = \log_e 0{\cdot}88$$
$$-0{\cdot}000124t = \log_e 0{\cdot}88$$
$$t = \frac{\log_e 0{\cdot}88}{-0{\cdot}000124}$$
$$= 1030{\cdot}914 \text{ (to 3 d.p.)}$$
$$> 1000.$$

So the claim is true.

12

(a) See **Straight Lines** §1
(b) See **Differentiation** §10

a i $PS = 6 - x$ and $RS = 12 - \frac{8}{x}$.

ii
$$\begin{aligned} A &= PS \times RS \\ &= (6-x)\left(12 - \frac{8}{x}\right) \\ &= 72 - \frac{48}{x} - 12x + 8 \\ &= 80 - 12x - \frac{48}{x}. \end{aligned}$$

b We have $1 \leq x \leq 4$. Extrema can occur at turning points or the endpoints of this closed interval.

Stationary points exist where $\frac{dA}{dx} = 0$.

$$A = 80 - 12x - 48x^{-1}$$

$$\frac{dA}{dx} = -12 + 48x^{-2} = 0$$

$$\frac{48}{x^2} = 12$$

$$x^2 = 4$$

$$x = \pm 2$$

$$x = 2 \text{ since } x > 0.$$

When $x = 1$, $A = 80 - 12 \times 1 - 48 = 20$.
When $x = 2$, $A = 80 - 12 \times 2 - \frac{48}{2} = 32$.
When $x = 4$, $A = 80 - 12 \times 4 - \frac{48}{4} = 20$.

So the minimum value of A is 20 when $x = 1, 4$ and the maximum value is 32 when $x = 2$.

2007 Paper 1

1

See **Straight Lines** §3 and §6

Method 1 $3x - y + 2 = 0$

$$y = 3x + 2$$

So $m = 3$.

> Remember: To extract the gradient, rearrange to the form $y = mx + c$.

Any line parallel to this has gradient 3.

The equation is $y - 4 = 3(x - (-1))$ using point $(-1, 4)$

$$y - 4 = 3x + 3$$

$$3x - y + 7 = 0.$$

Method 2 The equation of the line has the form $3x - y + c = 0$ and passes through $(-1, 4)$.

So $3(-1) - 4 + c = 0$

$$-7 + c = 0$$

$$c = 7.$$

So the line has equation $3x - y + 7 = 0$.

2

See **Vectors** §10

$$\overrightarrow{BC} = 2\overrightarrow{AB}$$

$$\underline{c} - \underline{b} = 2(\underline{b} - \underline{a})$$

> Remember: $\overrightarrow{AB} = \underline{b} - \underline{a}$

$$\underline{c} = 2\underline{b} - 2\underline{a} + \underline{b}$$

$$= 3\underline{b} - 2\underline{a}$$

$$= 3\begin{pmatrix} 1 \\ 3 \\ 2 \end{pmatrix} - 2\begin{pmatrix} -2 \\ 1 \\ -1 \end{pmatrix}$$

$$= \begin{pmatrix} 3 \\ 9 \\ 6 \end{pmatrix} - \begin{pmatrix} -4 \\ 2 \\ -2 \end{pmatrix}$$

$$= \begin{pmatrix} 7 \\ 7 \\ 8 \end{pmatrix}.$$ So C is the point $(7, 7, 8)$.

3

See **Functions and Graphs** §3

a $g(f(x)) = g(x^2+1) = 1-2(x^2+1) = 1-2x^2-2 = -1-2x^2.$

b $g(g(x)) = g(1-2x) = 1-2(1-2x) = 1-2+4x = 4x-1.$

4

See **Polynomials and Quadratics** §2

For no real roots, $b^2-4ac<0$ where $a=k, b=-1, c=-1$

$$(-1)^2-4k(-1)<0$$
$$1+4k<0$$
$$4k<-1$$
$$k<-\frac{1}{4}.$$

5

See **Circles** §3 and §1

Large circle centred at B: $x^2+y^2-14x-16y+77=0$

$2g=-14 \quad 2f=-16 \quad c=77.$

$g=-7 \quad f=-8$

Centre: $(-g,-f)=(7,8).$

Radius: $\sqrt{g^2+f^2-c} = \sqrt{49+64-77} = \sqrt{36} = 6$ units.

So each small circle has radius $\frac{6}{3}=2$ units.

Let D have coordinates $(x,8)$. Then since each small circle has radius 2, $x = 7+4\times2 = 15$. So D is $(15,8)$.

(The x-coord. of B.) (4 small radii.)

The circle centred at D has equation

$$(x-15)^2+(y-8)^2=4.$$

2007

6

See **Trigonometry** §5

$$\sin 2x^\circ = 6\cos x^\circ$$

$$2\sin x^\circ \cos x^\circ = 6\cos x^\circ$$

Using: $\sin 2A = 2\sin A\cos A$.

$$2\sin x^\circ \cos x^\circ - 6\cos x^\circ = 0$$

$$2\cos x^\circ(\sin x^\circ - 3) = 0$$

$$\cos x^\circ(\sin x^\circ - 3) = 0$$

$\cos x^\circ = 0$ or $\sin x^\circ - 3 = 0$

$x = 90, 270.$ $\quad\sin x^\circ = 3$

No solutions since $-1 \leq \sin x^\circ \leq 1$.

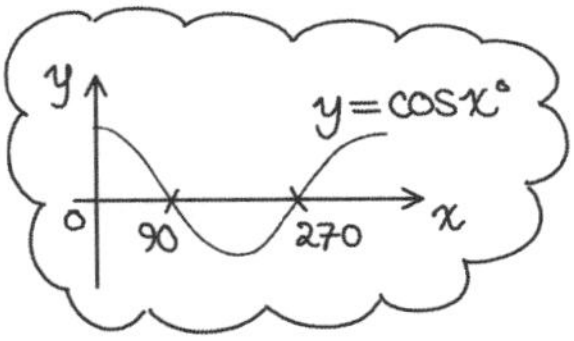

So $x = 90, 270$.

7

See **Sequences** – (a) §1 and §2, (b) §4

a $u_1 = \frac{1}{4}u_0 + 16 = \frac{1}{4} \times 0 + 16 = 16.$

$u_2 = \frac{1}{4}u_1 + 16 = \frac{1}{4} \times 16 + 16 = 4 + 16 = 20.$

$u_3 = \frac{1}{4} \times u_2 + 16 = \frac{1}{4} \times 20 + 16 = 5 + 16 = 21.$

b i The sequence has a limit because $-1 < \frac{1}{4} < 1$.

ii <u>Method 1</u> $\quad k = \frac{b}{1-a}$ where $a = \frac{1}{4}$ and $b = 16$.

$$k = \frac{16}{1 - 1/4} = \frac{16}{3/4} = \frac{4}{3} \times 16 = \frac{64}{3}.$$

<u>Method 2</u> As $n \to \infty$, $u_{n+1} = u_n = k$. So

$$k = \frac{1}{4}k + 16$$

$$\frac{3}{4}k = 16$$

$$k = \frac{4}{3} \times 16$$

$$= \frac{64}{3}$$

8

(a) and (b) See **Polynomials and Quadratics** *§9*
(c) See **Integration** *§5*

a Evaluate y when $x = 3$...

$$\begin{array}{r|rrrr} 3 & 1 & -4 & 1 & 6 \\ & & 3 & -3 & -6 \\ \hline & 1 & -1 & -2 & \boxed{0} \end{array}$$

OR

$$\begin{aligned} y &= 3^3 - 4 \times 3^2 + 3 + 6 \\ &= 27 - 36 + 9 \\ &= 0. \end{aligned}$$

So the curve crosses the x-axis at $(3, 0)$.

b Since $x = 3$ is a root, $(x - 3)$ is a factor.

$$\begin{aligned} \text{So } x^3 - 4x^2 + x + 6 &= (x-3)(x^2 - x - 2) \\ &= (x-3)(x+1)(x-2). \end{aligned}$$

Either from the bottom row of the table or by inspection.

So A has coordinates $(2, 0)$.

c The shaded area is

$$\begin{aligned} \int_0^2 (x^3 - 4x^2 + x + 6)\,dx &= \left[\frac{x^4}{4} - \frac{4x^3}{3} + \frac{x^2}{2} + 6x\right]_0^2 \\ &= \frac{2^4}{4} - \frac{4 \times 2^3}{3} + \frac{2^2}{2} + 6 \times 2 \\ &= 4 - \frac{32}{3} + 2 + 12 \\ &= 18 - 10\tfrac{2}{3} \\ &= 7\tfrac{1}{3} \text{ square units} \end{aligned}$$

(or $\frac{22}{3}$ square units.)

2007

9

See **Differentiation** §7, §8 and §9

a When $x = 0$, $f(0) = 3 \times 0 - 0^3 = 0$.

When $y = 0$, $3x - x^3 = 0$

$$x(3 - x^2) = 0$$

$$x = 0 \quad \text{or} \quad 3 - x^2 = 0$$

$$x = \pm\sqrt{3}.$$

So the curve passes through $(-\sqrt{3}, 0)$, $(0, 0)$ and $(\sqrt{3}, 0)$.

b Stationary points exist where $f'(x) = 0$.

$$f'(x) = 3 - 3x^2 = 0$$

$$x^2 = 1$$

$$x = \pm 1.$$

When $x = 1$, $y = 3 \times 1 - 1^3 = 3 - 1 = 2$. $(1, 2)$

When $x = -1$, $y = 3 \times (-1) - (-1)^3 = -3 + 1 = -2$. $(-1, -2)$.

<u>**Method 1**</u> Nature table...

x	-1^-	-1	-1^+	1^-	1	1^+
$f'(x)$	$-$	0	$+$	$+$	0	$-$
Sketch	╲	—	╱	╱	—	╲

<u>**Method 2**</u> The second derivative test... $f''(x) = -6x$.

$f(-1) > 0$, $f(1) < 0$.

So $(-1, -2)$ is a minimum turning point and $(1, 2)$ is a maximum turning point.

c

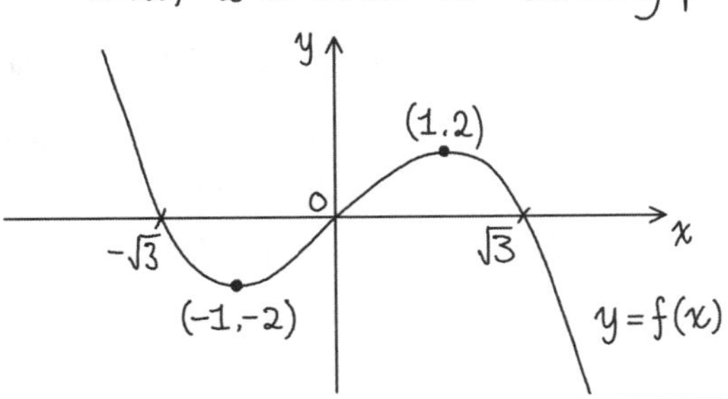

10

See **Further Calculus** §4

$$y = (3x^2 + 2)^{1/2}$$

$$\frac{dy}{dx} = \frac{1}{2}(3x^2 + 2)^{-1/2} \times \frac{d}{dx}(3x^2 + 2)$$

Remember the Chain Rule

$$= \frac{1}{2}(3x^2 + 2)^{-1/2} \times 6x$$

$$= \frac{3x}{\sqrt{3x^2 + 2}}.$$

11

See **Wave Functions** §6

a

$$\sqrt{3}\cos x + \sin x = k\cos(x - a)$$
$$= k\cos x \cos a + k \sin x \sin a$$
$$= (k\cos a)\cos x + (k \sin a)\sin x$$

Comparing coefficients:

$$k\sin a = 1$$
$$k\cos a = \sqrt{3}$$

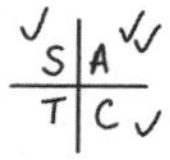

$$\begin{array}{c|c} \checkmark\,S & A\,\checkmark\checkmark \\ \hline T & C\,\checkmark \end{array}$$

So $k = \sqrt{1^2 + \sqrt{3}^2}$ and $\tan a = \dfrac{k\sin a}{k\cos a} = \dfrac{1}{\sqrt{3}}$.

$$= \sqrt{4}$$
$$= 2$$

$$a = \frac{\pi}{6}.$$

Exact value...

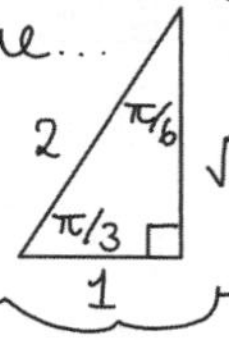

So $\sqrt{3}\cos x + \sin x = 2\cos\left(x - \dfrac{\pi}{6}\right)$.

b

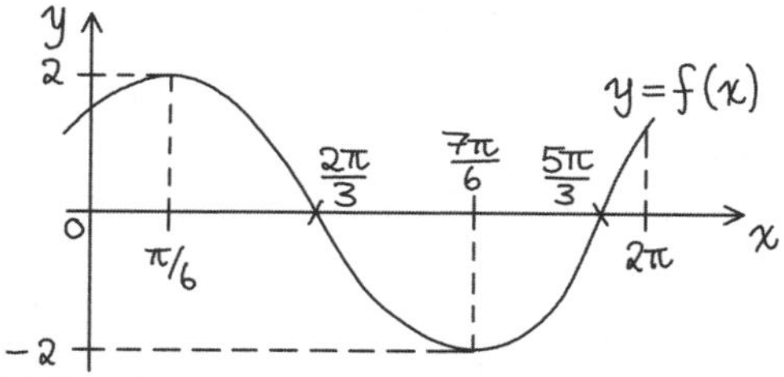

- The amplitude is 2.
- This is the graph of $y = 2\cos x$ shifted $\dfrac{\pi}{6}$ to the right.

2007 Paper 2

1

See **Vectors** §7 and §12

a $G(0,2,2)$.

b From the diagram

$$\underline{p} = \tfrac{1}{2}\underline{g} = \tfrac{1}{2}\begin{pmatrix}0\\2\\2\end{pmatrix} = \begin{pmatrix}0\\1\\1\end{pmatrix}.$$

$$\underline{q} = \underline{b} + \tfrac{1}{2}\overrightarrow{BG} = \underline{b} + \tfrac{1}{2}(\underline{g}-\underline{b}) = \tfrac{1}{2}(\underline{b}+\underline{g}) = \tfrac{1}{2}\begin{pmatrix}2\\4\\2\end{pmatrix} = \begin{pmatrix}1\\2\\1\end{pmatrix}.$$

c $|\underline{p}| = \sqrt{1^2+1^2} = \sqrt{2}$, $\quad |\underline{q}| = \sqrt{1^2+2^2+1^2} = \sqrt{6}$.

$\underline{p}\cdot\underline{q} = 0\times1 + 1\times2 + 1\times1 = 3$

So
$$\cos P\hat{O}Q = \frac{\underline{p}\cdot\underline{q}}{|\underline{p}||\underline{q}|} = \frac{3}{\sqrt{2}\sqrt{6}} = \frac{3}{2\sqrt{3}} = \frac{\sqrt{3}}{2}$$

Using: $\underline{a}\cdot\underline{b} = |\underline{a}||\underline{b}|\cos\theta$

Exact value...

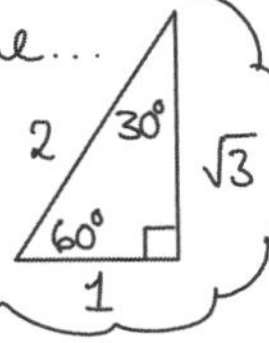

$$P\hat{O}Q = \cos^{-1}\left(\frac{\sqrt{3}}{2}\right) = 30° \quad \left(\text{or } \frac{\pi}{6} \text{ radians}\right)$$

2

See **Trigonometry** – (a) §3, (b) §4

Using Pythagoras's Theorem...

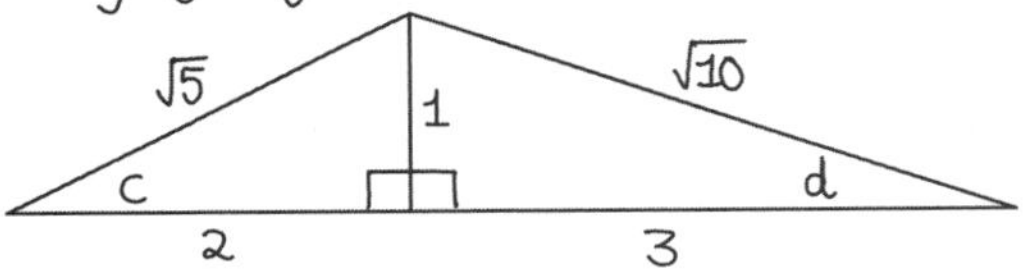

$\sin c = \frac{1}{\sqrt{5}} \quad \cos c = \frac{2}{\sqrt{5}}$

$\sin d = \frac{1}{\sqrt{10}} \quad \cos d = \frac{3}{\sqrt{10}}$

cont...

a $\sin(c+d) = \sin c.\cos d + \cos c \sin d$

$$= \frac{1}{\sqrt{5}} \times \frac{3}{\sqrt{10}} + \frac{2}{\sqrt{5}} \times \frac{1}{\sqrt{10}}$$

$$= \frac{3+2}{\sqrt{5}\sqrt{10}}$$

$$= \frac{5}{5\sqrt{2}}$$

$$= \frac{1}{\sqrt{2}}$$

b i $\sin 2c = 2\sin c \cos c = 2 \times \frac{1}{\sqrt{5}} \times \frac{2}{\sqrt{5}} = \frac{4}{5}.$

ii $\cos 2d = 2\cos^2 d - 1$

$$= 2 \times \frac{9}{10} - 1$$

$$= \frac{9}{5} - \frac{5}{5}$$

$$= \frac{4}{5}.$$

Any of the three formulae for cos2d could be used here.

3

See **Circles** §4

To find points of intersection, put $y = 6-2x$ into the equation of the circle:

$$x^2 + (6-2x)^2 + 6x - 4(6-2x) - 7 = 0$$

$$x^2 + 36 - 24x + 4x^2 + 6x - 24 + 8x - 7 = 0$$

$$5x^2 - 10x + 5 = 0$$

$$x^2 - 2x + 1 = 0$$

$$(x-1)^2 = 0$$

$$x = 1$$

You could also use the discriminant to show there is just one solution.

Since there is only one solution, the line is a tangent to the circle.

When $x = 1$, $y = 6 - 2 \times 1 = 4$.

So the point of contact is $(1,4)$.

2007

4

(a) See **Functions and Graphs** §9 and §10
(b) See **Trigonometry** §1

a The amplitude is 2, so $a = 2$.

There are three complete waves in $360°$ so $b = 3$.

The graph is the same as $y = a\sin(bx°)$ but shifted down 1.

So $c = -1$.

b $2\sin(3x°) - 1 = 0$

$\sin(3x°) = \frac{1}{2}$ $\begin{array}{c|c} \checkmark S & A \checkmark \\ \hline T & C \end{array}$

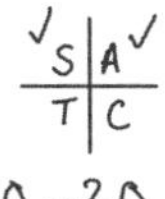

Exact value...

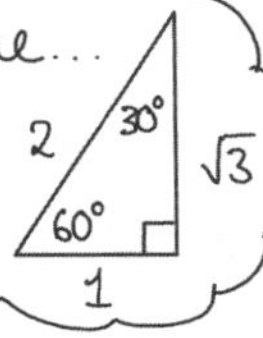

$3x = 30$ or $180 - 30$

$3x = 30$ or 150

$x = 10$ or 50

From the diagram, the x-coordinate of P is 50.

5

(a) See **Differentiation** §5 or **Polynomials and Quadratics** §7
(b) See **Polynomials and Quadratics** §7
(c) See **Circles** §6

a <u>Method 1</u> $\frac{dy}{dx} = 2 \times \frac{1}{2}x - 8 = x - 8$.

Remember:
$\frac{dy}{dx} = m_{tangent}$

$m_{tangent} = 4$ i.e. $\frac{dy}{dx} = 4$

So $x - 8 = 4$

$x = 12$.

When $x = 12$, $y = \frac{1}{2} \times 12^2 - 8 \times 12 + 34 = 72 - 96 + 34 = 10$

So Q is the point $(12, 10)$.

cont...

2007

Method 2 The tangent has the form $y = 4x + c$. There is just one point of intersection with the parabola.

So $\frac{1}{2}x^2 - 8x + 34 = 4x + c$

$\frac{1}{2}x^2 - 12x + 34 - c = 0$ has discriminant zero.

So $x = -\frac{b}{2a}$ where $a = \frac{1}{2}$, $b = -12$

$= \frac{12}{2 \times \frac{1}{2}} = 12.$

From the quadratic formula: $x = \frac{-b \pm \sqrt{b^2 - 4ac}}{2a}$

When $x = 12$, $y = \frac{1}{2} \times 12^2 - 8 \times 12 + 34 = 72 - 96 + 34 = 10.$

So Q is the point $(12, 10)$.

b P has the same y-coordinate as Q, so

$\frac{1}{2}x^2 - 8x + 34 = 10$ ← The y-coord. of P.

$\frac{1}{2}x^2 - 8x - 24 = 0$

$x^2 - 16x - 48 = 0$ multiplying through by 2.

$(x - 4)(x - 12) = 0$

$x = 4$ or $x = 12$.

So P is the point $(4, 10)$.

c C has x-coordinate 8 by symmetry.

Let C be the point $(8, y)$.

$m_{CQ} \times m_{tgt.} = -1$ since CQ is a radius.

So $m_{CQ} = -\frac{1}{4}$. However, $m_{CQ} = \frac{10 - y}{12 - 8} = \frac{10 - y}{4}$.

So $\frac{10 - y}{4} = -\frac{1}{4}$

$10 - y = -1$

$y = 11.$

So C is the point $(8, 11)$.

6 *See* **Differentiation** *§12 or* **Polynomials and Quadratics** *§3 and §1*

a i Using Pythagoras's Theorem: $ST = \sqrt{10^2 + 10^2} = \sqrt{200} = 10\sqrt{2}$.

ii

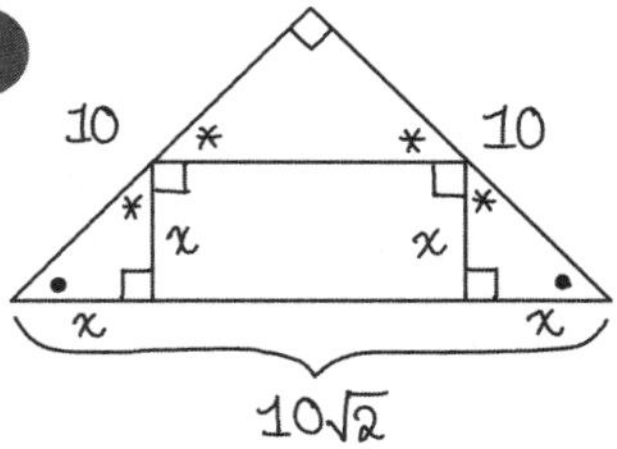

• = 45° since the large triangle is isosceles.

∗ = 45° since the angles in a triangle and on a straight line sum to 180°.

So the shaded area is $A = \text{length} \times \text{breadth}$

$$= (10\sqrt{2} - 2x)x$$

$$= 10\sqrt{2}x - 2x^2 \text{ square metres}$$

b Method 1 Stationary points exist where $\frac{dA}{dx} = 0$.

$$\frac{dA}{dx} = 10\sqrt{2} - 4x = 0$$

$$4x = 10\sqrt{2}$$

$$x = \frac{10\sqrt{2}}{4}$$

$$= \frac{5\sqrt{2}}{2}.$$

Nature...

x	$\frac{5\sqrt{2}}{2}^-$	$\frac{5\sqrt{2}}{2}$	$\frac{5\sqrt{2}}{2}^+$
$\frac{dA}{dx}$	+	0	−
Sketch	/	—	\

OR $\frac{d^2A}{dx^2} = -4$.

Hence $x = \frac{5\sqrt{2}}{2}$ gives the maximum area.

cont...

2007

Method 2 Completing the square...

$$A = -2x^2 + 10\sqrt{2}\,x$$
$$= -2(x^2 - 5\sqrt{2}\,x)$$
$$= -2\left(x - \frac{5\sqrt{2}}{2}\right)^2 + 2\left(\frac{5\sqrt{2}}{2}\right)^2$$

The x-coordinate of the turning point is $x = \frac{5\sqrt{2}}{2}$.

The turning point is a maximum since the x^2-coefficient is negative.

Hence $x = \frac{5\sqrt{2}}{2}$ gives the maximum area.

When the breadth is $\frac{5\sqrt{2}}{2}$ metres, the length is

$10\sqrt{2} - 2 \times \frac{5\sqrt{2}}{2} = 5\sqrt{2}$ metres.

7

See **Further Calculus** §6

$$\int_0^2 \sin(4x+1)\,dx$$
$$= \left[-\frac{1}{4}\cos(4x+1)\right]_0^2$$
$$= -\frac{1}{4}\cos(4\times2+1) + \frac{1}{4}\cos(4\times0+1)$$
$$= -\frac{1}{4}\cos 9 + \frac{1}{4}\cos 1$$
$$= 0.363 \quad \text{(to 3 d.p.)}$$

Using $\int \sin ax\,dx = -\frac{1}{a}\cos ax + c$.

Remember: We must work in radians when doing calculus.

2007

8

See **Exponentials and Logarithms** §5

Put $x = a$ and $y = 0$ into the equation:

$$0 = \log_3(a-1) - 2\cdot2$$

$$\log_3(a-1) = 2\cdot2$$

$$a - 1 = 3^{2\cdot2}$$

$$a = 3^{2\cdot2} + 1$$

$$= 12\cdot212 \quad \text{(to 3 d.p.)}$$

Remember: $x = \log_a y \Leftrightarrow a^x = y$

9

See **Exponentials and Logarithms** §7

a $y = a^{-x}$. Reflect in the y-axis.

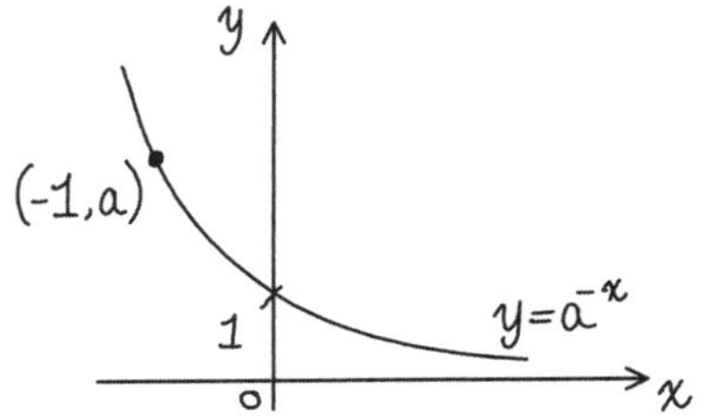

b $y = a^{1-x} = a \times a^{-x}$. The graph is as above but scaled by a in the y-direction — each y-coordinate is multiplied by $a > 0$.

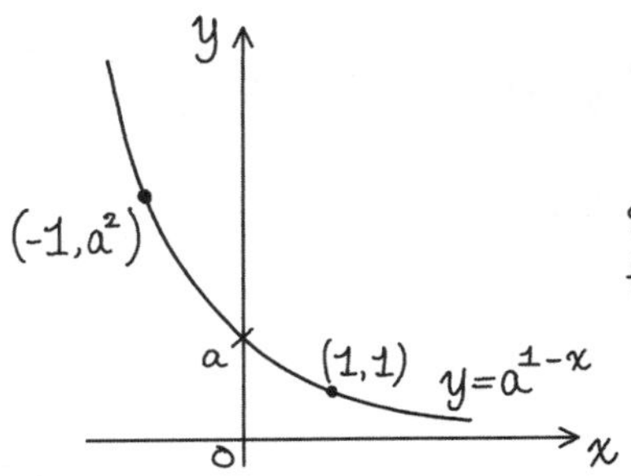

Also, when $x = 1$,

$$y = a^{1-1} = a^0 = 1.$$

So the curve passes through the point $(1, 1)$.

10

(a) See **Polynomials and Quadratics** *§5*
(b) See **Integration** *§3*

a i The curve $y = f'(x)$ has roots $x = 2$ and $x = 4$. So $x-2$ and $x-4$ are factors of $f'(x)$.
So $a = 2$ and $b = 4$ (or vice versa).

ii We know that $f'(0) = 6$, so

$$k(0-4)(0-2) = 6$$
$$8k = 6$$
$$k = \frac{6}{8}$$
$$= \frac{3}{4}.$$

b
$$f(x) = \int f'(x)\,dx$$
$$= \frac{3}{4}\int (x-2)(x-4)\,dx$$
$$= \frac{3}{4}\int (x^2 - 6x + 8)\,dx$$
$$= \frac{3}{4}\left(\frac{x^3}{3} - 3x^2 + 8x\right) + c$$

From the question, $f(0) = 6$. So $c = 6$. Therefore:

$$f(x) = \frac{3}{4}\left(\frac{x^3}{3} - 3x^2 + 8x\right) + 6 = \frac{1}{4}x^3 - \frac{9}{4}x^2 + 6x + 6.$$

11

See **Exponentials and Logarithms** *– (a) and (b) §5, (c) §6*

a Put $x = a$ and $y = 6$ in the equation:

$$6 = 3 \times 4^a$$
$$4^a = 2$$
$$a = \frac{1}{2} \text{ since } 4^{1/2} = \sqrt{4} = 2.$$

cont...

b Put $x = -\frac{1}{2}$ and $y = b$ in the equation:

$$b = 3 \times 4^{-1/2}$$
$$= \frac{3}{\sqrt{4}}$$
$$= \frac{3}{2}.$$

Remember: $u^{-m} = \frac{1}{u^m}$.

c <u>Method 1</u> $y = 3 \times 4^x$

$$\log_{10} y = \log_{10}(3 \times 4^x) \quad \text{taking } \log_{10} \text{ on both sides}$$
$$= \log_{10} 3 + \log_{10} 4^x$$
$$= \log_{10} 3 + x \log_{10} 4$$

Remember:
- $\log_a xy = \log_a x + \log_a y$.
- $k \log_a x = \log_a x^k$

So $\log_{10} y = (\log_{10} 4)x + \log_{10} 3$

The gradient is $\log_{10} 4$. (Comparing to $y = mx + c$.)

<u>Method 2</u> Start with $\log_{10} y = Px + Q$ and find P and Q.

$$\log_{10} y = Px + Q$$
$$y = 10^{Px+Q}$$
$$y = 10^Q \times 10^{Px}$$

Comparing to $y = 3 \times 4^x \ldots$

$10^Q = 3$ and $10^{Px} = 4^x$

$Q = \log_{10} 3$ $\qquad (10^P)^x = 4^x$

$10^P = 4$

$P = \log_{10} 4.$

The gradient is $P = \log_{10} 4$.

2007

SQP Paper 1

1

See **Differentiation** §2

$$y = \frac{x^3 - x}{x^2} = \frac{x^3}{x^2} - \frac{x}{x^2} = x - x^{-1}.$$

$$\frac{dy}{dx} = 1 + x^{-2} = 1 + \frac{1}{x^2}.$$

Remember: $\frac{x^a}{x^b} = x^{a-b}$.

B

2

See **Functions and Graphs** §3

$$g(f(x)) = g(2x-3) = (2x-3)^2 = 4x^2 - 12x + 9.$$

A

3

See **Integration** §1 and §2

$$\int \frac{1}{\sqrt[3]{x}}\,dx = \int x^{-1/3}\,dx$$

$$= \frac{x^{2/3}}{2/3} + c$$

$$= \frac{3}{2}x^{2/3} + c$$

Remember: $\frac{a}{b/c} = a \times \frac{c}{b}$

C

4

See **Vectors** §3

$$d_{AB}^2 = (2-(-1))^2 + (3-(-4))^2 + (-2-0)^2$$

$$= 3^2 + 7^2 + (-2)^2$$

$$= 9 + 49 + 4$$

$$= 62.$$

So $d_{AB} = \sqrt{62}$.

C

5

See **Sequences** §1 and §2

$u_0 = -1$

$u_1 = 3u_0 - 4 = 3 \times (-1) - 4 = -3 - 4 = -7.$

$u_2 = 3u_1 - 4 = 3 \times (-7) - 4 = -21 - 4 = -25.$

A

6

See **Functions and Graphs** §10

$y = -3 - f(x) = -f(x) - 3.$

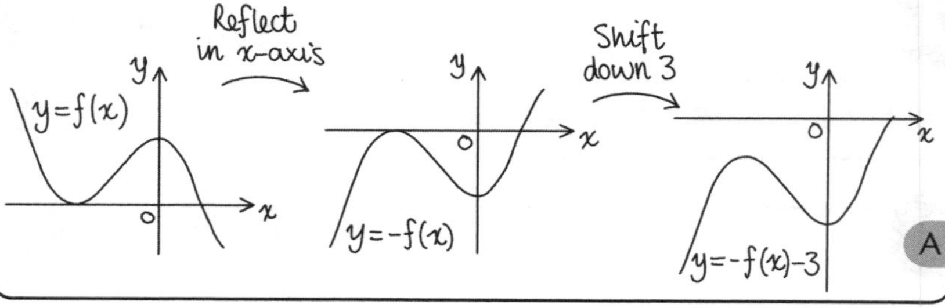

A

7

See **Polynomials and Quadratics** §3 and §1

The turning point is $(4, -5)$.
Since the x^2 coefficient is $3 > 0$,
the parabola is concave up, i.e.
$\cup$-shaped.
So the turning point is a minimum.

Remember:
The parabola $y = a(x-p)^2 + q$ has turning point (p, q).

C

8

See **Trigonometry** §4

$$\sin 2x^\circ = 2\sin x^\circ \cos x^\circ = 2 \times \frac{2\sqrt{2}}{3} \times \frac{1}{3} = \frac{4\sqrt{2}}{9}$$

$$\sin x^\circ = \frac{\text{opposite}}{\text{hypotenuse}} = \frac{2\sqrt{2}}{3}.$$

$$\cos x^\circ = \frac{\text{adjacent}}{\text{hypotenuse}} = \frac{1}{3}.$$

A

SQP

9

See **Trigonometry** §3

$\sin a = \frac{\text{opp.}}{\text{hyp.}} = \frac{1}{\sqrt{5}}$

$\cos a = \frac{\text{adj.}}{\text{hyp.}} = \frac{2}{\sqrt{5}}$

$\sin b = \frac{1}{\sqrt{17}}$, $\cos b = \frac{4}{\sqrt{17}}$

$$\begin{aligned}\sin(a-b) &= \sin a\cos b - \cos a \sin b \\ &= \frac{1}{\sqrt{5}} \times \frac{4}{\sqrt{17}} - \frac{2}{\sqrt{5}} \times \frac{1}{\sqrt{17}} \\ &= \frac{4-2}{\sqrt{5}\sqrt{17}} \\ &= \frac{2}{\sqrt{85}}\end{aligned}$$

Remember: $\sqrt{x}\sqrt{y} = \sqrt{xy}$

B

10

See **Circles** §3

The radius is $\sqrt{g^2+f^2-c}$ where $g=4$, $f=-3$ and $c=-12$.

i.e. $\sqrt{4^2+(-3)^2-(-12)} = \sqrt{16+9+12} = \sqrt{37}$.

C

11

See **Vectors** §9

Since points P, Q and R are collinear, $\overrightarrow{QR} = k\overrightarrow{PQ}$ for some constant k.

$$\overrightarrow{PQ} = \underset{\sim}{q} - \underset{\sim}{p} = \begin{pmatrix}5\\13\\13\end{pmatrix} - \begin{pmatrix}1\\3\\7\end{pmatrix} = \begin{pmatrix}4\\10\\6\end{pmatrix}$$

$$\overrightarrow{QR} = \underset{\sim}{r} - \underset{\sim}{q} = \begin{pmatrix}s\\33\\25\end{pmatrix} - \begin{pmatrix}5\\13\\13\end{pmatrix} = \begin{pmatrix}s-5\\20\\12\end{pmatrix}$$

So each component of $\overrightarrow{QR}$ is twice the component of $\overrightarrow{PQ}$

$$\begin{aligned}\text{So}\quad s-5 &= 2\times 4 \\ s &= 8+5 \\ s &= 13.\end{aligned}$$

C

SQP

12

See **Polynomials and Quadratics** §3

Method 1 $2x^2 - 12x + 11 = 2(x^2 - 6x) + 11$

$= 2(x-3)^2 - 18 + 11$

$= 2(x-3)^2 - 7$. So $c = -7$.

Method 2 Comparing coefficients...

$2x^2 - 12x + 11 = 2(x-b)^2 + c$

$= 2(x^2 - 2bx + b^2) + c$

$= 2x^2 - 4bx + 2b^2 + c$.

So $4b = 12$ and $2b^2 + c = 11$

$b = 3$.

$c = 11 - 2 \times 3^2$

$c = 11 - 18$

$c = -7$.

B

13

See **Integration** §3

$y = \int \frac{dy}{dx}\, dx$

$= \int (3x^2 + 9x + 1)\, dx$

$= \frac{3x^3}{3} + \frac{9x^2}{2} + x + c$

$= x^3 + \frac{9}{2}x^2 + x + c$.

The curve passes through the origin, so $y = 0$ when $x = 0$.

Hence $c = 0$ and so $y = x^3 + \frac{9}{2}x^2 + x$.

A

14

See **Polynomials and Quadratics** §2

For equal roots, $b^2 - 4ac = 0$ where $a = 1$, $b = -3$ and $c = k$.

$$(-3)^2 - 4 \times 1 \times k = 0$$
$$9 - 4k = 0$$
$$k = \frac{9}{4}.$$

D

15

See **Circles** §6

The centre of the circle is (3,4).

So $m_{radius} = \frac{4-2}{3-(-1)} = \frac{2}{4} = \frac{1}{2}$

$\therefore m_{tgt} = -2$ since the radius and tangent are perpendicular.

A

16

See **Further Calculus** §6

$$\int_0^{\pi/6} (4\cos 2x)\,dx = \left[4 \times \tfrac{1}{2}\sin 2x\right]_0^{\pi/6}$$
$$= \left[2\sin 2x\right]_0^{\pi/6}$$
$$= 2\sin\tfrac{\pi}{3} - 2\sin 0$$
$$= 2 \times \tfrac{\sqrt{3}}{2} - 0$$
$$= \sqrt{3}.$$

Using: $\int \cos ax\,dx = \frac{1}{a}\sin ax + c$.

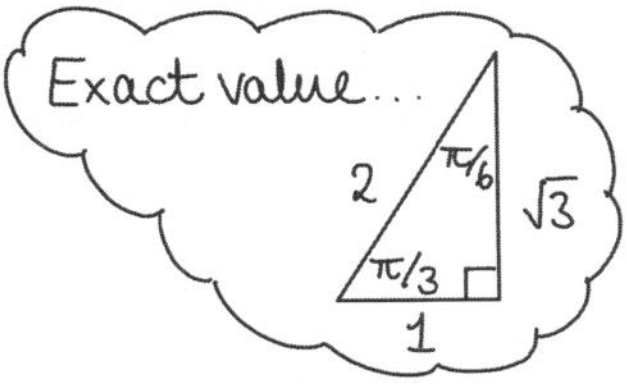

C

17

See **Functions and Graphs** §9 and §10

There are 2 complete waves in 2π radians, so $p = 2$.

The graph is $y = \sin(2x)$ shifted up 1, so $q = 1$.

A

SQP

18

See **Vectors** §11 and §13

The angle ϑ between $\underline{a}$ and $\underline{c}$ is such that $\cos\vartheta = \frac{\text{adj.}}{\text{hyp.}} = \frac{3}{5}$.

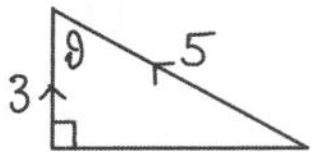

So $\underline{a}.\underline{c} = |\underline{a}||\underline{c}|\cos\vartheta = 3 \times 5 \times \frac{3}{5} = 9$. So (1) is true.

Since $\underline{a}$ and $\underline{b}$ are perpendicular, $\underline{a}.\underline{b} = 0$. So (2) is false.

B

19

See **Exponentials and Logarithms** §5

<u>Method 1</u>

$$\log_3 t - \log_3 5 = 2$$
$$\log_3\left(\frac{t}{5}\right) = 2$$
$$\frac{t}{5} = 3^2$$
$$t = 5 \times 9$$
$$= 45$$

Remember:
- $\log_a x - \log_a y = \log_a \frac{x}{y}$.
- $y = \log_a x \Leftrightarrow x = a^y$.

<u>Method 2</u>

$$\log_3 t = 2 + \log_3 5$$
$$= 2\log_3 3 + \log_3 5$$
$$= \log_3 3^2 + \log_3 5$$
$$= \log_3 (9 \times 5)$$
$$= \log_3 45$$
$$t = 45.$$

Remember:
- $\log_a a = 1$
- $\log_a x + \log_a y = \log_a xy$
- $\log_a x = \log_a y \Leftrightarrow x = y$

D

20

See **Exponentials and Logarithms** §5

$$3^k = e^4$$
$$\log_e 3^k = \log_e e^4 \quad \text{taking } \log_e \text{ on both sides}$$
$$k \times \log_e 3 = 4$$
$$k = \frac{4}{\log_e 3}.$$

Remember:
- $\log_a x^k = k\log_a x$
- $\log_a a = 1$

C

21

See **Sequences** §2 and §4

a Product A: $u_{n+1} = 0{\cdot}3u_n + 300$ $u_0 = k$, a constant

($0{\cdot}3$: 70% of the germs are removed, so 30% remain.)

Product B: $v_{n+1} = 0{\cdot}2v_n + 350$ $v_0 = k$.

b As $n \to \infty$, u_n and v_n both tend to limits because $-1 < 0{\cdot}3 < 1$ and $-1 < 0{\cdot}2 < 1$.

<u>Method 1</u>

$$l_A = \frac{300}{1-0{\cdot}3} = \frac{300}{0{\cdot}7} = \frac{3000}{7}.$$

$$l_B = \frac{350}{1-0{\cdot}2} = \frac{350}{0{\cdot}8} = \frac{3500}{8}.$$

<u>Method 2</u> As $n \to \infty$, $u_{n+1} = u_n = l_A$ and $v_{n+1} = v_n = l_B$.

$$l_A = 0{\cdot}3l_A + 300 \qquad l_B = 0{\cdot}2l_B + 350$$

$$0{\cdot}7l_A = 300 \qquad 0{\cdot}8l_B = 350$$

$$l_A = \frac{300}{0{\cdot}7} \qquad l_B = \frac{350}{0{\cdot}8}$$

$$= \frac{3000}{7} \qquad = \frac{3500}{8}$$

To compare, put over a common denominator:

$$l_A = \frac{3000}{7} = \frac{3000 \times 8}{56} = \frac{24\,000}{56}$$

$$l_B = \frac{3500}{8} = \frac{3500 \times 7}{56} = \frac{24\,500}{56}$$

So $l_A < l_B$.

<u>OR</u> carry out division:

A: $7\overline{)3000{\cdot}000}$ = $428{\cdot}571$ so the number of germs present will settle around 428.

B: $8\overline{)3500{\cdot}0}$ = $437{\cdot}5$ so the number of germs present will settle around 437.

So product A is more effective in the long term.

22

*See **Differentiation** §7, §8 and §9*

a Stationary points exist where $\frac{dy}{dx} = 0$.

$$\frac{dy}{dx} = 3x^2 - 18x + 24 = 0$$

$$x^2 - 6x + 8 = 0 \quad (\div 3)$$

$$(x-2)(x-4) = 0.$$

$$x - 2 = 0 \quad \text{or} \quad x - 4 = 0$$

$$x = 2 \qquad\qquad x = 4.$$

When $x = 2$, $y = 2^3 - 9 \times 2^2 + 24 \times 2 - 20$

$= 8 - 36 + 48 - 20$

$= 0. \quad (2,0)$

Or use synthetic division.

When $x = 4$, $y = 4^3 - 9 \times 4^2 + 24 \times 4 - 20$

$= 64 - 9 \times 16 + 96 - 20$

$= 140 - 144$

$= -4 \quad (4,-4).$

Method 1 Nature table:

x	2^-	2	2^+	4^-	4	4^+
$(x-2)$	$-$	0	$+$	$+$		$+$
$(x-4)$	$-$		$-$	$-$	0	$+$
$\frac{dy}{dx}$	$+$	0	$-$	$-$	0	$+$
Sketch	/	—	\	\	_	/

Method 2 Second derivative test: $\frac{d^2y}{dx^2} = 6x - 18.$

When $x = 2$, $\frac{d^2y}{dx^2} = -6 < 0$. When $x = 4$, $\frac{d^2y}{dx^2} = 6 > 0$.

So $(2,0)$ is a maximum turning point.

$(4,-4)$ is a minimum turning point.

cont...

SQP

b i $(x-2)^2(x-5) = (x^2-4x+4)(x-5)$

$= x^3 - 4x^2 + 4x - 5x^2 + 20x - 20$

$= x^3 - 9x^2 + 24x - 20.$

ii To find the x-axis intercepts, put $y=0$:

$x^3 - 9x^2 + 24x - 20 = 0$

$(x-2)^2(x-5) = 0$

$x-2=0$ or $x-5=0$

$x=2$ $\quad x=5.$

So the curve passes through $(2,0)$ and $(5,0)$.

To find the y-axis intercept, put $x=0$: $y=-20$.

So the curve passes through $(0,-20)$.

Using this information and the stationary points:

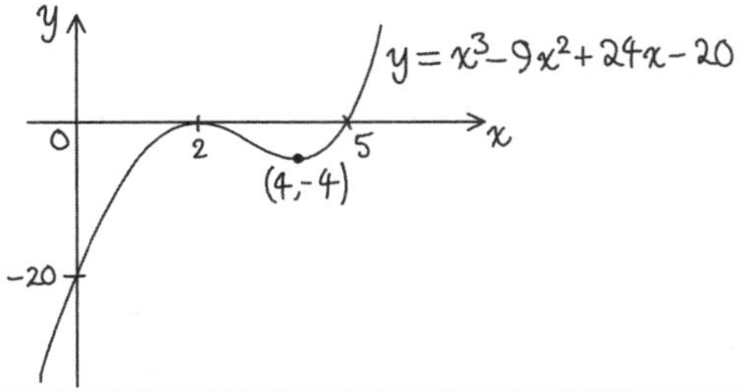

23 See **Polynomials and Quadratics** *§11 and §9*

Equate to find points of intersection...

$x^3 + 5x^2 - 36x + 32 = -x^2 + x + 2$

$x^3 + 6x^2 - 37x + 30 = 0.$

cont...

Method 1 By inspection: $(x-1)(x^2+7x-30)=0$

$(x-1)(x+10)(x-3)=0$

$x=1$ or $x=-10$ or $x=3$.

Method 2 Evaluate the expression for $x=1$:

1	1	6	−37	30
		1	7	−30
	1	7	−30	0

Since the remainder is 0, $x=1$ is a root so $(x-1)$ is a factor.

$x^3+6x^2-37x+30=0$

$(x-1)(x^2+7x-30)=0$

The coefficients of the other factor come from the bottom row of the table.

$(x-1)(x+10)(x-3)=0$.

$x=1$ or $x=-10$ or $x=3$.

From the diagram, A has $x=-10$, B has $x=1$ and C has $x=3$

24

See **Trigonometry** §5

$\sin^2 p - \sin p + 1 = 1 - \sin^2 p$

$2\sin^2 p - \sin p = 0$

$\sin p(2\sin p - 1) = 0$

Remember:
$\sin^2 x + \cos^2 x = 1$
so $\cos^2 x = 1 - \sin^2 x$

$\sin p = 0$ or $2\sin p - 1 = 0$

$p = ~~0, \pi, 2\pi~~$

We want $\frac{\pi}{2} < p < \pi$

$\sin p = \frac{1}{2}$

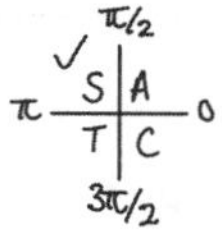

We want $\frac{\pi}{2} < p < \pi$.

$p = \pi - \frac{\pi}{6}$

$= \frac{5\pi}{6}$.

Exact value...

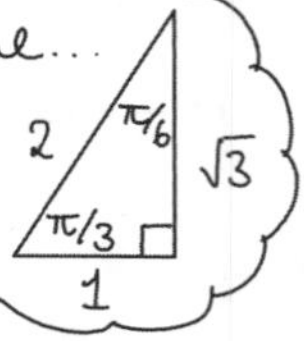

So $p = \frac{5\pi}{6}$.

SQP Paper 2

1

See **Straight Lines** (a) §7, (b) §8, (c) §10, (d) §3

a $N = \text{midpoint}_{AB} = \left(\frac{2+10}{2}, \frac{1+1}{2}\right) = (6,1).$

$m_{CN} = \frac{1-7}{6-4} = \frac{-6}{2} = -3.$

So the equation is $y - 1 = -3(x-6)$ using $N(6,1)$

$$y - 1 = -3x + 18$$

$$3x + y - 19 = 0.$$

b $m_{BC} = \frac{7-1}{4-10} = \frac{6}{-6} = -1$. So $m_{AD} = 1$ since $AD \perp BC$.

(i.e. $m_{BC} \times m_{AD} = -1$)

So the equation is $y - 1 = 1(x-2)$ using $A(2,1)$.

$$x - y - 1 = 0.$$

c Solve simultaneously...

__Method 1__ Eliminating y:

$$3x + y - 19 = 0 \quad \text{——} (1)$$

$$x - y - 1 = 0 \quad \text{——} (2)$$

$(1)+(2)$: $4x - 20 = 0$

$$x = 5$$

__Method 2__ Rearrange both equations for y and equate:

$$19 - 3x = x - 1$$

$$4x = 20$$

$$x = 5$$

When $x = 5$, $y = 5 - 1 = 4$. So P has coordinates $(5,4)$.

d $m_{PQ} = \frac{1-4}{8-5} = \frac{-3}{3} = -1 = m_{BC}$ from part (b).

So PQ and BC are parallel.

SQP

2

See **Vectors** §7, §3 and §12

a The lengths of the edges are as follows...

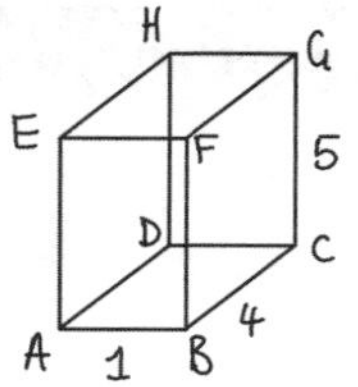

- A and B only differ in the first coordinate, so the length of AB is the difference in the first coordinate.
- Similar for BC = AD.
- G has coordinates (2,7,9) so GC = AE = 5.

Note: It's not necessary to show any of this working.

So AB = 1, AD = 4, AE = 5.

b $\overrightarrow{HB} = \underline{b} - \underline{h} = \begin{pmatrix}2\\3\\4\end{pmatrix} - \begin{pmatrix}1\\7\\9\end{pmatrix} = \begin{pmatrix}1\\-4\\-5\end{pmatrix}.$

$\overrightarrow{HC} = \underline{c} - \underline{h} = \begin{pmatrix}2\\7\\4\end{pmatrix} - \begin{pmatrix}1\\7\\9\end{pmatrix} = \begin{pmatrix}1\\0\\-5\end{pmatrix}.$

Remember: $\overrightarrow{AB} = \underline{b} - \underline{a}$

You could just write these down from the diagram.

$|\overrightarrow{HB}| = \sqrt{1^2 + (-4)^2 + (-5)^2} = \sqrt{42}.$

$|\overrightarrow{HC}| = \sqrt{1^2 + (-5)^2} = \sqrt{26}.$

Method 1

$$\cos B\hat{H}C = \frac{\overrightarrow{HB}.\overrightarrow{HC}}{|\overrightarrow{HB}||\overrightarrow{HC}|}$$

$$= \frac{1\times 1 - 4\times 0 - 5\times(-5)}{\sqrt{42}\sqrt{26}}$$

Using: $\underline{a}.\underline{b} = |\underline{a}||\underline{b}|\cos\theta$

$$B\hat{H}C = \cos^{-1}\left(\frac{26}{\sqrt{42}\sqrt{26}}\right)$$

$$= 38\cdot 11^\circ \text{ (to 2 d.p.)}$$

OR $0\cdot 665$ rads (to 3 d.p.)

cont...

SQP

Method 2 We have:

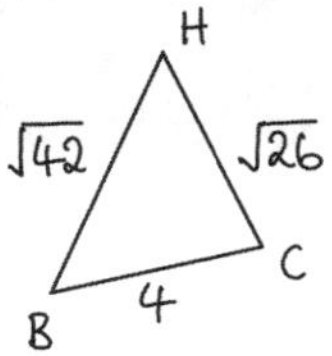

So $\cos B\hat{H}C = \dfrac{42+26-16}{2\sqrt{42}\sqrt{26}}$

$= \dfrac{26}{\sqrt{42}\sqrt{26}}$

Remember the cosine rule: $\cos A = \dfrac{b^2+c^2-a^2}{2bc}$

So $B\hat{H}C = 38{\cdot}11°$ (to 2 d.p.) OR $0{\cdot}665$ rads (to 3 d.p.)

3

See **Wave Functions** §2 and §5

a $5\sin x° - 12\cos x° = k\sin(x° - a°)$

$= k\sin x°\cos a° - k\cos x°\sin a°.$

$= (k\cos a°)\sin x° - (k\sin a°)\cos x°.$

Comparing coefficients: $k\sin a° = 12$, $k\cos a° = 5$

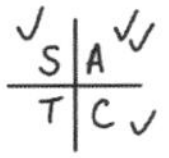

So $k = \sqrt{12^2+5^2}$ and $\tan a° = \dfrac{k\sin a°}{k\cos a°} = \dfrac{12}{5}$

$= \sqrt{169}$

$= 13$

$a = \tan^{-1}\left(\frac{12}{5}\right) = 67{\cdot}38$ (to 2 d.p.)

So $5\sin x° - 12\cos x° = 13\sin(x° - 67{\cdot}38°)$.

b $5\sin x° - 12\cos x° = 6{\cdot}5$

$13\sin(x° - 67{\cdot}38°) = 6{\cdot}5$

$\sin(x° - 67{\cdot}38°) = 0{\cdot}5$

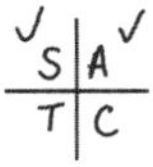

$\sin^{-1}(0{\cdot}5) = 30°$

$x - 67{\cdot}38 = 30$ or $180 - 30$

$x = 97{\cdot}38$ or $217{\cdot}38$ (to 2 d.p.)

4

(a) See ***Differentiation*** *§5*
(b) See ***Circles*** *§5*
(c) See ***Vectors*** *§10*

a $\frac{dy}{dx} = 4x - 2.$ (Remember: $\frac{dy}{dx} = m_{tangent}$)

When $x = 1$, $m_{tangent} = 4 \times 1 - 2 = 2$.

Using P(1,3), the equation is $y - 3 = 2(x - 1)$

$$y - 3 = 2x - 2$$
$$2x - y + 1 = 0.$$

b Put $y = 2x + 1$ into the equation of the circle...

$$x^2 + (2x+1)^2 + 8(2x+1) + 11 = 0$$
$$x^2 + 4x^2 + 4x + 1 + 16x + 8 + 11 = 0$$
$$5x^2 + 20x + 20 = 0$$
$$x^2 + 4x + 4 = 0$$
$$(x+2)^2 = 0$$
$$x = -2.$$

(You could have used the discriminant to show that there is only one solution)

Since there is only one solution, there is only one point of intersection. Hence the line is a tangent to the circle.

When $x = -2$, $y = 2 \times (-2) + 1 = -4 + 1 = -3$.
So the point of contact is $Q(-2, -3)$.

cont...

c QP has equation $y = 2x + 1$.
So when $x = 0$, $y = 1$.

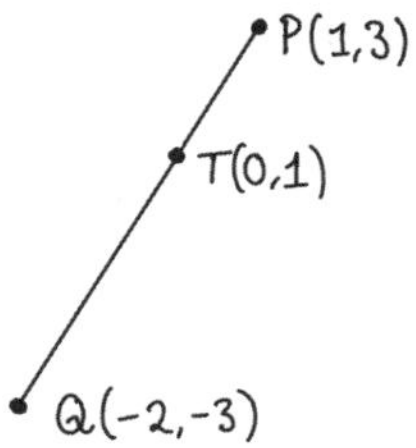

Method 1

$\overrightarrow{TP} = \begin{pmatrix} 1 \\ 2 \end{pmatrix}$, $\overrightarrow{QT} = \begin{pmatrix} 2 \\ 4 \end{pmatrix} = 2\overrightarrow{TP}$

So T divides $\overrightarrow{QP}$ in the ratio 2:1.

Method 2

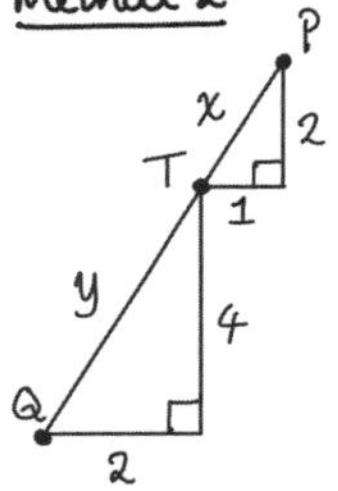

By Pythagoras's Theorem:

$x^2 = 2^2 + 1^2$, so $x = \sqrt{5}$.

$y^2 = 4^2 + 2^2$, so $y = \sqrt{20} = 2\sqrt{5}$.

So T divides $\overrightarrow{QP}$ in the ratio 2 : 1.

5

(a) See **Integration** *§6*
(b) See **Differentiation** *§12 or* **Polynomials and Quadratics** *§3*

a Points of intersection...

$$x^2 = 6x + 16$$

$$x^2 - 6x - 16 = 0$$

$$(x+2)(x-8) = 0$$

$$x + 2 = 0 \quad \text{or} \quad x - 8 = 0.$$

$$x = -2 \qquad x = 8$$

cont...

SQP

The shaded area is given by

$$\int_{-2}^{8} (\text{upper} - \text{lower})\, dx$$

$$= \int_{-2}^{8} (6x + 16 - x^2)\, dx$$

$$= \left[3x^2 + 16x - \frac{x^3}{3}\right]_{-2}^{8}$$

$$= \left(3 \times 8^2 + 16 \times 8 - \frac{8^3}{3}\right) - \left(3 \times (-2)^2 + 16 \times (-2) - \frac{(-2)^3}{3}\right)$$

$$= \frac{448}{3} + \frac{52}{3}$$

$$= \frac{500}{3} \quad \left(= 166\tfrac{2}{3}\right).$$

So the area is $\frac{500}{3}$ square units.

b We want to maximise $A(x) = -5x^2 + 30x + 80$.

<u>Method 1</u> Stationary points exist where $A'(x) = 0$.

$$A'(x) = -10x + 30 = 0$$

$$x = \frac{30}{10}$$

$$= 3$$

Then $A(3) = -5 \times 3^2 + 30 \times 3 + 80 = 125$.

Nature:

x	3^-	3	3^+
$A'(x)$	+	0	−
Sketch	/	—	\

So the maximum area is 125 square units.

cont...

Method 2 Completing the square...

$$A(x) = -5(x^2 - 6x) + 80$$
$$= -5(x-3)^2 + 45 + 80$$
$$= -5(x-3)^2 + 125.$$

The turning point is $(3, 125)$ and is a maximum since $-5 < 0$ so the parabola is concave down ($\cap$).

So the maximum area is 125 square units.

As a proportion of the total area it is $\frac{125}{500/3} = \frac{375}{500} = \frac{3}{4}$.

6

See **Exponentials and Logarithms** §5

a

$$A(1600) = \tfrac{1}{2}A_0$$ After 1600 years, the amount has halved.

$$A_0 e^{-1600k} = \tfrac{1}{2}A_0$$
$$e^{-1600k} = \tfrac{1}{2}$$
$$-1600k = \log_e\left(\tfrac{1}{2}\right)$$ Taking $\log_e$ on both sides

$$k = -\frac{\log_e\left(\frac{1}{2}\right)}{1600}$$
$$= 0.0004332 \text{ (to 4 s.f.)}$$

b **Method 1** $A(3200) = A_0 \times e^{(-0.0004332 \times 3200)}$

$= 0.250A_0$ (to 3 d.p.)

Remember the brackets on your calculator.

So after 3200 years, we are left with 25%.

Method 2 Let $A_0 = 100$ since we start with 100%.

Then $A(3200) = 100e^{(-0.0004332 \times 3200)}$

$= 25.001$ (to 3 d.p.)

$= 25$ (to the nearest whole number)

So after 3200 years, we are left with 25%.

SQP

7

See **Trigonometry** §4

From the diagram, $\cos 2x° = \frac{\text{adj.}}{\text{hyp.}} = \frac{6}{10} = \frac{3}{5}$.

$$\cos 2x° = 2\cos^2 x° - 1 = \frac{3}{5}$$

$$2\cos^2 x° = \frac{8}{5}$$

$$\cos^2 x° = \frac{8}{10}$$

$$\cos^2 x = \frac{4}{5}$$

$$\cos x° = \pm\frac{2}{\sqrt{5}}.$$

Since x is acute, $\cos x° > 0$ so $\cos x° = \frac{2}{\sqrt{5}}$.

From the diagram, $\cos x° = \frac{6}{BD}$

$$BD = \frac{6}{2/\sqrt{5}}$$

$$= 3\sqrt{5} \text{ units.}$$

SQP